SCHOLASTIC

Reading Skills
Chills & Thrills

**Spine-Tingling Tales With Comprehension Questions
That Help Kids Identify the Main Idea, Draw Conclusions,
Determine Cause and Effect, and More**

by DAN GREENBERG

D1530726

NEW YORK • TORONTO • LONDON • AUCKLAND • SYDNEY
MEXICO CITY • NEW DELHI • HONG KONG • BUENOS AIRES

Teaching Resources

Cover design by Maria Lilja
Illustrations by Jack Desrocher
Interior design by Holly Grundon
Edited by Denise Rinaldo

ISBN 0-439-43765-2
Copyright © 2005 by Dan Greenberg
All rights reserved.
Printed in the U.S.A.

1 2 3 4 5 6 7 8 9 10   40   13 12 11 10 09 08 07 06 05

Contents

Introduction 4

Tale No. 1:
The Bijou Ghost 6
Reading for Details

Tale No. 2:
Love Potion Commotion 9
Cause and Effect

Tale No. 3:
The Next Step: Scare Radio 12
Main Idea

Tale No. 4:
The Toothbrush 15
Compare and Contrast

Tale No. 5:
The Ugly Druckling 18
Point of View

Tale No. 6:
The Horrible Green Creature 21
Drawing Conclusions

Tale No. 7:
The House on Plum Street 24
Analyzing Plot

Tale No. 8:
The Hideous Blob's
Amazing Comeback 27
Main Idea and Supporting Details

Tale No. 9:
The Butcher and His Wife 30
Making Inferences

Tale No. 10:
The Three Ghosts of Lucy Bly 33
Understanding Character

Tale No. 11:
Ask Aunt Doty: An Advice Column for
the Supernaturally Inclined 36
Author's Purpose

Tale No. 12:
The Choice 39
Making Predictions

Tale No. 13:
A Really Bad Hair Day 42
Reading for Details

Tale No. 14:
Ratkins! 45
Understanding Setting

Tale No. 15:
Tales From the Telephone:
True Horror 48
Author's Purpose

Tale No. 16:
Problems Facing Young People Today:
An Editorial by Maxwell Bile 51
Fact vs. Opinion

Tale No. 17:
The Dirt: A Horror World
Gossip Column 54
Compare and Contrast

Tale No. 18:
Nasty Little Monster 57
Sequence of Events

Tale No. 19:
The Ghost Who Didn't Believe 60
Cause and Effect

Answer Key 63

Skills Index 64

Introduction

Ghosts and monsters, spooks and creatures, groaning, moaning, creepy-crawly blobs of slime—could anything be more fun for kids in grades 3 to 6? How about having your horror with a twist of humor, a dash of silliness, and a healthy dose of rock-solid reading skills instruction?

FunnyBone Books: Reading Skills Chills & Thrills pairs humorous horror stories (for student appeal) with related exercises designed to build important reading skills (for teacher appeal). Though all of the tales are creepy and funny, they are far from identical. They cover a variety of writing styles and genres—from radio script to newspaper editorial to gossip column to classic-style horror story.

Each of the 19 reproducible stories focuses on a particular reading skill, such as author's purpose, cause and effect, making inferences, and predicting. The stories and accompanying skills exercises will help students grow in the key areas of

- reading comprehension,
- critical thinking,
- problem solving,
- logical analysis,
- creative writing,
- creative thinking, and
- test taking.

The tales and exercises are designed to help you and your students meet the twelve standards for the English Language Arts set forth by International Reading Association and National Council of Teachers of

English. *Reading Skills Chills & Thrills* can also be used to prepare students for standardized tests, which assess the very skills that the stories reinforce.

Each reproducible story is designed to teach a particular reading skill. Seven multiple-choice questions—all keyed to the story's skill—accompany each tale. The last question is a writing prompt that links to the story and the skill. For a complete index of all the reading and writing skills in this book, please refer to page 64. An answer key is on page 63.

How to Use This Book

The goal of this book is to use humor and horror to make reading skills less frightening and more fun for students. There are many ways to go about it. Here are some ideas:

1. BY READING SKILL: Choose stories according to the key reading skill you wish to cover. See the Skills Index on page 64.

2. BY WRITING SKILL: Choose stories according to the key writing skill you wish to cover. See the Skills Index on page 64.

3. AS AN INTERACTIVE CLASSROOM ACTIVITY:
   • Read the stories aloud as a class.
   • Have students read in pairs or small groups.
   • Have students work cooperatively to answer the questions and complete the writing exercises.

4. AS A WRITING PROMPT: Go beyond the suggested writing activities with these extension ideas:
   • Have students write prequels or sequels to the stories.
   • Have students rewrite the stories from various points of view.
   • Have students try writing their own stories in the various genres and styles presented in the book.

5. AS INSPIRATION FOR A CLASS PROJECT: Work as a group to create your own hauntingly humorous stories and exercises, or invent a unique reading-skill horror character for your classroom.

6. JUST FOR FUN: Let students choose how and when to read the stories on their own.

The Bijou Ghost

A **Reading for Details** Spooky Story

Little things mean a lot. That old saying is definitely true when you're reading! To be good reader, you have to pay attention to small **details**. The trick is figuring out which details are important to the story. Also, you have to understand how all the details hook together. Try it in this tale of a friendly ghost with an interesting hobby.

Once upon a time there was a young specter named Jasper. Jasper was a well-behaved phantom. He had a nice ghostly glow. He was good at haunting and spooking. And he really enjoyed moaning and groaning.

Jasper's one big problem was that he loved movies. And this brought him too close to human beings.

"Stay away from people," Jasper's mother always told him. "They're nothing but trouble."

For the most part, Jasper did stay away. He spent his time haunting a beautiful old movie theater named the Bijou.

For years, the Bijou was the most popular theater in town. The big old place had worn velvet seats, a giant screen, and an old-fashioned balcony. The popcorn was topped with real butter. But then the Multi-Plex 18 was built next door at the local mall. The Multi-Plex had bad popcorn and small screens. But it was new and it had a big parking lot. Everyone wanted to go there instead of the Bijou—well, everyone but Jasper. Like many ghosts, he hated new buildings and refused to haunt them.

Before long, the Bijou was nearly empty most nights. Phyllis, the manager, started thinking about selling the theater to a dog-food company. It got so bad that one night not a single person came to the 8 P.M. show. So, rather than hide up in the rafters, Jasper felt free to soar around in the drafty old theater and howl while he watched the movie.

"A-A-A-A-O-O-O-O!"

This was a big mistake.

Because what Jasper forgot was that Mike, the young projectionist, was still in the theater.

"What the—" Mike shrieked. "There's a ghost up there!"

Jasper tried to hide, but he couldn't avoid being seen by Phyllis, the manager, and Teresa, the popcorn lady. Before long, the police, newspaper reporters, TV cameras, and a whole host of gawkers had arrived to see the "Bijou Ghost." In fact, the theater was almost full.

To avoid being seen again, Jasper had to shrink himself down into a very uncomfortable size and shape and hide until the movie ended. While he was hiding, Jasper couldn't help overhearing people in the audience say such things as "What a beautiful theater!" and, "I just love this place!" and, "This is so much better than the Multi-Plex!"

This gave Jasper an idea. He was sad that the theater was losing customers. If it closed, he'd have nowhere to haunt. This could be his chance to do something about it! The following night, when no more than a dozen customers came to watch the movie, he waited until just the right moment, and suddenly let out a ghostly moan.

"A-ROOOO-O-O-O-O-O!!!!!"

"Did you hear that?" people cried.

Within minutes, the police, newspapers, and cameras once again arrived. This time an even bigger crowd of gawkers came with them.

"Where's the ghost?" they all cried.

Jasper played it cool. To keep them all guessing, he stayed hidden until the movie was over. But now the word was out. The following night, a long line formed outside of the Bijou.

"What's going on?" asked Mike.

"They've come to see the ghost," said Phyllis.

It was true. The people had come to see Jasper. But by the time the show was half over, they were enjoying the movie so much that they'd forgotten about the ghost.

1. **Jasper's favorite thing in the world is**
   - ○ **A.** ghosts.
   - ○ **B.** people.
   - ○ **C.** movies.
   - ○ **D.** popcorn.

2. **What was the one thing that Jasper's mother told him to stay away from?**
   - ○ **A.** Ghosts
   - ○ **B.** People
   - ○ **C.** The movies
   - ○ **D.** Popcorn

3. **The Bijou Theater is in danger of closing because**
   - ○ **A.** the building is too dilapidated to repair.
   - ○ **B.** it is haunted.
   - ○ **C.** it sells popcorn with real butter.
   - ○ **D.** customers are going to the newer theater.

4. **Why didn't Jasper haunt the Multi-Plex?**
   - ○ **A.** It was too far away.
   - ○ **B.** It did not have velvet seats.
   - ○ **C.** It was too new.
   - ○ **D.** It was too old.

This pattern continued. At first, people came just to get a glimpse of the "Bijou Ghost." But after they came once, they didn't even care about the ghost anymore. They came for the theater. Before long, the Bijou was once again the most successful theater in the county. Simply put, it was the best place to watch a movie anywhere!

"I couldn't agree more!" Jasper cried.

To this day, Jasper still stays up there, haunting the Bijou Theater. He hardly ever moans anymore or flies across the ceiling when people are around. But he does like to munch popcorn during the movie. So, if you're sitting in the Bijou, you might hear a quiet crunching and feel a few kernels spilling down from above. That's Jasper, the ghost, up in the rafters.

THE END

5. **Why did so many people come to the Bijou Theater?**
   ○ **A.** To see a movie
   ○ **B.** Because the Multi-Plex was closed
   ○ **C.** To see the ghost
   ○ **D.** Because it was less expensive

6. **What did many people notice when they came to the Bijou?**
   ○ **A.** That they really liked Jasper
   ○ **B.** That they really liked the theater
   ○ **C.** That they really liked the candy
   ○ **D.** That the theater was dirty

7. **How did Jasper help save the Bijou?**
   ○ **A.** He got the other ghosts to stop haunting it.
   ○ **B.** He helped the owners fix it up.
   ○ **C.** He held a fundraiser.
   ○ **D.** He attracted customers to the theater.

8. **You're an author and you're writing a guidebook to haunted places in the United States. Write a one-paragraph entry for the Bijou Theater, describing the ghostly goings-on that have been reported there.**

Love Potion Commotion

A **Cause and Effect** Spooky Story

All things happen for a reason—even spooky scary things. The **effect** is the thing that happens. The **cause** is the reason for the effect. See how it works in this story.

T he moral of this story is always to finish your homework before you go out to have fun. So if you're doing homework right now, for goodness' sake, finish it before you start this story!

What happened was this: A young man named Greg was working on his science-fair project. Now, this wasn't just any old science project. That would be too dull for Greg. He was the kind of person who always wanted to do something totally different.

"Actually, I'm making a love potion," Greg explained to his best friend Jeff.

"Why a love potion?" Jeff asked. "Do you want to fall in love?"

"Not really," Greg said. "I made some hate potion. But it seemed too nasty. So I switched to love potion. I call it Love Potion Number 5."

"Fascinating!" exclaimed Jeff. "So, now that you're finished, let's do something really interesting. Let's go to Fun Land." Fun Land was an amusement park that had lots of rides and costume-wearing characters.

Greg put the potion safely in his jacket pocket and off they went. When they got to Fun Land, the first thing they did was go on the Super Looper, the world's most loopy roller coaster.

"Whoa!" Greg screamed, as they went completely upside down.

Little did he know that the love potion in his pocket had become uncorked and was spraying down on Fun Land below.

When Greg and Jeff got off the ride, they saw all of the princesses, pixies, swans, and other costumed characters looking oddly at them.

"Hey, honey," the Magic Princess said to Greg. "You're a doll!"

"Huh?" Greg said.

"Greg, honey," called the Queen of the Swans. "Come on over here, sweetheart."

"What?" Greg said.

Then all of the other princesses, pixies, swans, and others came running up.

"They're after us!" cried Greg.

"Not us," said Jeff. "They're after you!"

1. **EFFECT: Greg made love potion.**
   CAUSE:
   ○ **A.** Greg wanted to have an unusual project for the science fair.
   ○ **B.** Greg was in love with a girl at school.
   ○ **C.** Jeff was in love with a girl at school.
   ○ **D.** Greg wanted to get rich.

2. **CAUSE: Greg went upside down in the Super Looper.**
   EFFECT:
   ○ **A.** Greg felt like he was going to throw up.
   ○ **B.** Greg fell in love with the Magic Princess.
   ○ **C.** The characters fell in love with Greg and Jeff.
   ○ **D.** The love potion spilled.

3. **CAUSE: The love potion splashed on the Magic Princess.**
   EFFECT:
   ○ **A.** She fell in love with Jeff.
   ○ **B.** Greg fell in love with her.
   ○ **C.** She fell in love with Greg.
   ○ **D.** Her gown was ruined.

4. **EFFECT: The costumed characters chased after Greg.**
   CAUSE:
   ○ **A.** The characters wanted some love potion.
   ○ **B.** Greg forgot that the love potion was in his pocket.
   ○ **C.** The characters were in love with Greg.
   ○ **D.** The characters were angry with Greg.

And with that, Jeff, not such a loyal best friend, hightailed it out of there. That left Greg to fend for himself against the horde of love-struck admirers.

"Help!" Greg cried, and ran to the first ride he could find. It turned out to be the Tunnel of Love!

Quickly, Greg jumped into a Love Boat with his admirers chasing hotly behind. It was then that he realized he still had a bottle of his original science-fair project—the hate potion—in his other pocket. If he sprinkled a little of the hate potion on his admirers, maybe that would block the effects of the love potion.

To do this, he needed to get high above them all. So, like a swashbuckling hero, Greg got out of his car and climbed high above the Tunnel of Love.

"Oh, look!" his adorers cried. "He's climbing up there!"

"He's so handsome!" they swooned.

"He's such a hero!" they pined.

"I love him!" they declared.

And then, *P-H-H-H-T-T!* Greg sprayed the hate potion down below. Suddenly, the admirers found that their love had cooled.

"What are we doing here?" they asked.

"He's not really so handsome," they declared.

"He's actually sort of creepy," one of them said.

And with that, Greg made his escape. He went directly home and finished his homework. Except, instead of making a love potion for his science-fair project, he did a dull old plant experiment instead—and he was glad he did!

THE END

---

5. **CAUSE: Jeff wasn't a very loyal friend.**
   EFFECT:
   ○ **A.** Jeff left Greg at the amusement park to fend for himself.
   ○ **B.** Greg left Jeff at the amusement park to fend for himself.
   ○ **C.** Jeff helped Greg escape from the characters who were chasing him.
   ○ **D.** Jeff copied Greg's science-fair project.

6. **EFFECT: Greg sprayed hate potion on the characters who were chasing him.**
   CAUSE:
   ○ **A.** He wanted them to hate each other.
   ○ **B.** He wanted them to stop being in love with him.
   ○ **C.** He hated them.
   ○ **D.** Greg went upside down in the roller coaster.

7. **EFFECT: The characters fell out of love with Greg.**
   CAUSE:
   ○ **A.** The love potion canceled out the effects of the hate potion.
   ○ **B.** The hate potion was not effective.
   ○ **C.** The hate potion canceled out the effects of the love potion.
   ○ **D.** The love potion wore off on its own.

8. You're a magazine ad writer. On a separate sheet of paper, write an ad for Love Potion Number 5. Be sure to describe the potion's effects, and the things that would make a person to want to buy it. Include pictures if you like.

The Next Step: Scare Radio

A **Main Idea** Spooky Story

This transcript from a spooky radio show gives you a rare peek into the everyday life of otherworldly creatures. Read it with the lights on! While you read, look for the **main idea**—or key message—that each character is trying to express.

List of Characters

SPOOK	**BLOB**
PANEL MEMBERS	**JESSICA**
BRUNHILDA	**GHOSTLY FIGURE**

SPOOK: Hello! I'm Spook Specter, host of *The Next Step*, the award-winning radio show that each week investigates the weird, wild, and wacky world of the supernatural. Today's topic is: "Are Ghosts Real?" For thousands of years, people have argued about this topic. Today, we'll try to settle it once and for all. Now it's time to introduce our panel. Hello, panel.

PANEL MEMBERS: Hello, Spook.

SPOOK: Our first panel member is Brunhilda Hagstrom, professor of paranormal sorcery at Witch Haven College. Tell me, Brunhilda, are ghosts real?

BRUNHILDA: Hello, darling. The answer to your question is yes! But, I must say, it's rather a boring question! Who cares about ghosts? Why the other day, I was mixing up a batch of Love Potion when I thought I saw a ghost, and—

SPOOK: Really? So you're convinced ghosts are real? Fascinating!

BRUNHILDA: Fascinating? It was disgusting! Ghosts are vile, dirty, noisy, irritating creatures! When I see one I quickly grab my broom and sweep it out the door! This happens at least twice a day in my laboratory at the college.

SPOOK: Amazing, Brunhilda! Just amazing. Our next panelist is last year's Creature of the Year. Yes, it's none other than the Toxic Blob, the creature from the radioactive swamp. Hello, Blobbie!

BLOB: How are you doing, Spook? If you ask me, ghosts can't be real. Know why? To be real, you've got to be solid, you know? You've got to have form and shape. Ghosts ain't got those. Have you ever punched a ghost in the kisser? There's nothing there! Your hand goes right through it!

SPOOK: Hmm, that may be true, Blobbie. But tell me this: You yourself are a formless, shapeless, gooey hulk. So how are you any more real than a ghost?

BLOB: *(feels himself)* Whoa! You got a good point there, Spook. I never thought of it that way.

SPOOK: Fascinating. Our final panelist is Jessica, the Teenage Zombie. Jess hasn't been the same since she was bored to the breaking point when her friends forced her to sit through the movie *Creepy Teenage Prom Night*. So what about it, Jess? Are ghosts real?

JESSICA: Nothing is real, Spook. I mean, take the sun. It rises in the morning. It sets at night. But is it real? Everything is an illusion, Spook, including ghosts.

SPOOK: So I take it you don't believe in ghosts.

JESSICA: What I believe isn't important, Spook. Only the truth is important. And . . . hey, what's that?

A strange, glowing, half-transparent figure suddenly hovers over the room.

JESSICA: Is that what I think it is?

BLOB: Yow! I'm getting out of here. That thing gives me the creeps.

BRUNHILDA: Don't be silly. Ghosts are annoying—not dangerous.

JESSICA: Look out!

BLOB: It's coming after us! I think it's mad!

GHOSTLY FIGURE: *O-o-o-o-o-o . . . .*

SPOOK: That's all for now for *The Next Step*. Tune in next week when we discuss, "Is Poison Really Bad for You?" Until then, so long from your host, Spook Specter.

THE END

1. **What is the main idea of the show called *The Next Step*?**
   - ◯ **A.** To scare the audience
   - ◯ **B.** To explain why ghosts aren't real
   - ◯ **C.** To explore the world of the supernatural
   - ◯ **D.** To sell exercise equipment

2. **What is the main idea of this week's show?**
   - ◯ **A.** To meet all of the panelists
   - ◯ **B.** To discuss whether ghosts are real
   - ◯ **C.** To prove that ghosts are disgusting
   - ◯ **D.** To discuss radio shows

3. **What main idea does Brunhilda express?**
   - ◯ **A.** That she doesn't believe in ghosts
   - ◯ **B.** That she doesn't like ghosts
   - ◯ **C.** That ghosts aren't solid
   - ◯ **D.** That she loves ghosts

4. **What main idea does the Blob express?**
   - ◯ **A.** That ghosts aren't solid enough to be real
   - ◯ **B.** That ghosts are vile, disgusting creatures
   - ◯ **C.** That ghosts are dangerous
   - ◯ **D.** That blobs are intelligent

5. **What details does the Blob use to support his idea?**
   - ◯ **A.** That ghosts make him laugh
   - ◯ **B.** That ghosts don't exist
   - ◯ **C.** That no one has form or shape
   - ◯ **D.** That ghosts don't have form or shape

6. **What main idea does Jessica express?**
   - ◯ **A.** That nothing is real
   - ◯ **B.** That ghosts are real
   - ◯ **C.** That ghosts are not real
   - ◯ **D.** That ghosts are not scary

7. **What detail at the end of the show supports the idea that ghosts are real?**
   - ◯ **A.** Brunhilda describes a ghost she once met.
   - ◯ **B.** Spook shows a movie of a ghost.
   - ◯ **C.** The host turns out to be a ghost.
   - ◯ **D.** A ghostly figure appears.

8. **On a separate sheet of paper, make a list of three main ideas for future episodes of *The Next Step*. Be as wild and imaginative as you like! Choose one of your ideas, then write Spook's introduction for that show.**

The Toothbrush

A **Compare and Contrast** Spooky Story

Yes, it's true. Your bathroom is home to billions of tiny bacteria. And don't forget that each one of them is a living thing! Read this icky story, then **compare and contrast** bacteria life to human life. Remember, when you compare, you show how two things are alike. When you contrast, you show how two things are different.

It was bedtime, but Billy Bacteria was not tired at all. "Tell me another story, Mom," Billy begged.

"Now, Billy," his mother said. "You know that if I tell you too many stories, I won't have enough time to tell stories to all of your other 35 billion brothers and sisters."

"Aw, come on, Mom. Just one more story?" Billy pleaded. "And make it a spooky one."

Billy's mom loved Billy very much, so she told him another story—a very spooky story.

"There was once a happy little bacterium," she began.

"Was he like me, Mom?" Billy asked.

"Yes," she said, "he was a lot like you, Billy. This little bacterium had a great life. He was part of a large scum ring on the side of a nice big bathroom sink. Every day he played in the water with his bacteria friends. They had a lot of fun together, but this didn't stop the little bacterium from dreaming about the future."

"What did he dream about, Mom?"

"Oh," said his mom, "his dreams were pretty much like everyone else's dreams. He wanted to grow up and be part of an infection."

"Wow!" Billy cried. "An infection! That's just like Dad. Do you think I could be an infection some day, Mom?"

"Well," she chuckled, "not all by yourself. But if you got together with a few billion of your good friends, why not?"

"Wow!" Billy said. "So what happened next?"

1. **Compare Billy to characters in typical children's stories. In what way is he similar?**
   - ○ **A.** He lives under the sink and dreams of becoming part of an infection.
   - ○ **B.** He seems to be a nice kid with a nice family.
   - ○ **C.** He has billions of brothers and sisters.
   - ○ **D.** He goes to school.

2. **In what way does Billy's family differ from families in typical children's stories?**
   - ○ **A.** His mother tells him bedtime stories.
   - ○ **B.** Instead of a few brothers and sisters, he has billions of brothers and sisters.
   - ○ **C.** Instead of going to bed at night, he goes to bed in the daytime.
   - ○ **D.** His mother has to take care of more than one child.

3. **Compare Billy's life to the life of a character in a typical children's story. Find similarities.**
   - ○ **A.** Both have friends and dream of the future.
   - ○ **B.** Both play football and baseball.
   - ○ **C.** Both live on the side of a sink.
   - ○ **D.** Both want to be part of an infection.

4. **Contrast Billy's life to the life of typical children's story characters. Find differences.**
   - ○ **A.** Billy loves to play with his friends and wants to go to college.
   - ○ **B.** Billy dreams of being like his dad.
   - ○ **C.** Billy lives on the side of a sink instead of a house.
   - ○ **D.** Billy lives in a house instead of an apartment.

"What always happens?" replied Billy's mom. "One moment the little bacterium was getting ready for bed, and the next thing you know a big fat toothbrush swooped down on him."

"A toothbrush!" Billy cried. "What's a toothbrush, Mom?"

"A toothbrush," she explained, "is a very scary thing. First of all, it's gigantic. In fact, a toothbrush is said to be so big that you can't even see it in a microscope!"

"Oh come on," Billy said, now obviously scared out of his wits. "That can't be true. Does Dad believe in toothbrushes, Mom?"

"I'm not sure," Billy's mom said. "What I do know is that a toothbrush is said to move up and down, smashing and dislodging trillions of innocent bacteria wherever it goes. And that's not even the scary part."

Now Billy was shaking in his boots. But he was enjoying the story nevertheless.

"W-w-what's the scary part, Mom?"

"The scary part," she said, "is that the toothbrush is covered with a horrible white, foamy goop called TOOTHPASTE, and this toothpaste is specially made to DESTROY bacteria like you and me."

By now, Billy was so scared he was shaking. But this didn't prepare him for what happened next: He looked up and saw a REAL toothbrush about to come down right on top of them.

"Look out!" Billy's mom cried.

The user of the toothbrush must have been shaking it off. It knocked hard against the sink, dislodging some of the scum ring where Billy lived.

A rush of water whooshed them out of there just in time. Billy and his mom came to a new home under the sink. It was very dark and safe there. And there were no toothbrushes to be seen anywhere.

Billy loved his new home. But it was quite a while before he wanted his mom to tell him another spooky story again—especially one about a toothbrush!

THE END

5. **Which of the following does Billy have in common with many human kids?**
   - ○ **A.** He likes to listen to bedtime stories.
   - ○ **B.** He likes to listen to stories about toothbrushes.
   - ○ **C.** He likes to make up stories about toothbrushes and toothpaste.
   - ○ **D.** He likes to live under the sink.

6. **Contrast the spooky story that Billy's mom tells with spooky bedtime stories humans tell. What is different about the story that Billy's mom tells?**
   - ○ **A.** It has a monster in it that scares the listener.
   - ○ **B.** The monster is huge and dangerous.
   - ○ **C.** The monster is a toothbrush.
   - ○ **D.** The monster is friendly.

7. **What similarity do the characters in this story share with characters in traditional monster stories?**
   - ○ **A.** They know how to defeat the monster.
   - ○ **B.** They are not sure that the monster in the story really exists.
   - ○ **C.** They ignore the danger that the monster presents.
   - ○ **D.** They are afraid of toothbrushes.

8. **Choose a character from one of your favorite books or stories. Write a paragraph comparing and contrasting your life to the life of the character.**

The Ugly Druckling

A **Point of View** Spooky Story

Your **point of view** is your way of looking at things. To you, a big buzzing fly is a pest. But from the point of view of a frog, that fly is a tasty treat! Of course, when you change, it can cause you to see things differently. That means you have a new point of view. See how it works in this strange story.

nce upon a time there was an Ugly Druckling. What's a *druckling*? Druckling is a nickname for a type of caterpillar, not a bird. In fact, drucklings are rather wormy, ugly-looking things. But to a druckling, ugly isn't bad. It's good. So the other drucklings didn't make fun of the Ugly Druckling. They were jealous of her because they wanted to be as ugly as she was.

"Why does she get to be so ugly?" they would say. "We're so plain!"

It just didn't seem fair.

And then, wouldn't you know it, there was a fancy ball that was hosted by an Ugly Prince. The Ugly Prince fell deeply in love with the Ugly Druckling right away.

"I've never seen anyone so ugly before," he said, when she ran from the ball at midnight. "I must find out who she is."

The next day, the Ugly Prince went looking for the Ugly Druckling, but he couldn't find her anywhere.

The Ugly Prince found himself at the edge of a forest. In frustration, he cried out, "Where are you, Ugly Druckling?"

A voice replied, "Here I am, Ugly Prince."

The prince looked around. He quickly realized that the voice was that of a beautiful butterfly—not the Ugly Druckling he'd fallen in love with. What had happened? During the night, the Ugly Druckling had changed into a Beautiful Butterfly. (This was something that happened to all drucklings. It would happen to the prince, too. But since drucklings are not members of a highly intelligent species—like us, humans— they didn't quite get it.)

The prince covered his face in horror.

"You're beautiful!" he exclaimed.

"Yes," she said. "But inside I'm as ugly as ever. And anyway, I now understand that being ugly isn't the most important thing in life. Do you still love me?"

"Hmm," the Ugly Prince said. "Let me get back to you on that. I'll call you tonight."

---

1. **How does the point of view of drucklings toward beauty differ from what you might expect?**
   - ○ **A.** Drucklings think beauty is a bad thing.
   - ○ **B.** Drucklings think beauty is wonderful.
   - ○ **C.** Drucklings think personality is more important than beauty.
   - ○ **D.** Drucklings prize beauty above all else.

2. **What is the prince's point of view toward the Ugly Druckling when he meets her at the ball?**
   - ○ **A.** She is his heart's desire.
   - ○ **B.** She is a troublemaker.
   - ○ **C.** She is frightening.
   - ○ **D.** She is disgusting.

3. **How has the Ugly Druckling's point of view changed?**
   - ○ **A.** She now sees things from a prince's point of view.
   - ○ **B.** She now sees things from a human's point of view.
   - ○ **C.** She now sees things from the point of view of a beautiful butterfly.
   - ○ **D.** She now sees things from a duck's point of view.

4. **After she changes, the Ugly Druckling sees that looking ugly is**
   - ○ **A.** the most important thing in life.
   - ○ **B.** frightening.
   - ○ **C.** very difficult.
   - ○ **D.** not as important as she once thought.

But the prince didn't call. All of the other drucklings laughed.

"What's the matter?" they teased. "Doesn't your Ugly Prince love you anymore?"

"Yes, he does," said the Ugly Druckling (who was now a Beautiful Butterfly). "He knows that I may be beautiful on the outside, but inside I'm still as ugly as ever. And that's what matters."

She insisted that the prince would be there any moment. But sometimes princes aren't as noble and brave as they're supposed to be. All night the Ugly Druckling (who was now a Beautiful Butterfly) waited. The Ugly Prince still didn't call.

Finally, in the morning, she went to the garden, and there she met up with another beautiful butterfly.

"Who are you?" the Ugly Druckling asked.

"Don't you recognize me?" replied the butterfly. "I'm the Ugly Prince that you met at the ball."

"But you're so beautiful," she said.

"Yes," he said. "Last night I, too, went through metamorphosis. That's why I didn't call you. I was busy turning into a butterfly."

"Hmm," the Ugly Druckling said.

"You know," said the prince, "I have a confession to make. Yesterday when you told me that you were still ugly on the inside I didn't really believe you. But now I do."

"Why is that?" asked the Ugly Druckling (who was now a Beautiful Butterfly).

"I'm not sure," said the Ugly Prince (who was now a Handsome Prince). "But I think it has something to do with my point of view. Do you still love me?"

"I think I do," replied the Ugly Druckling (who was now a Beautiful Butterfly). "Do you still love me?"

"Yes," said the Ugly Prince (who was now a Handsome Prince). "There is something ugly about your beauty. But the way you look isn't that important."

"I know what you mean," said the Ugly Druckling (who was now a Beautiful Butterfly).

So, they got married and lived happily ever after. They had dozens of caterpillar kids. And they were all ugly!

THE END

---

5. **Why didn't the Ugly Druckling recognize the Ugly Prince when they met in the garden?**
    - ○ **A.** He was wearing different clothes.
    - ○ **B.** He had changed into a butterfly.
    - ○ **C.** He had changed into a caterpillar.
    - ○ **D.** Her way of seeing things had changed.

6. **The Ugly Prince changed into a butterfly, but he felt the same as ever on the inside. This helped him understand that**
    - ○ **A.** the Ugly Druckling hadn't changed on the inside.
    - ○ **B.** butterflies are beautiful.
    - ○ **C.** drucklings are ugly.
    - ○ **D.** the Ugly Druckling really loved him.

7. **How did the point of view of both main characters change by the end of the story?**
    - ○ **A.** They didn't like the way drucklings look.
    - ○ **B.** They couldn't see anymore.
    - ○ **C.** They both saw that what's on the inside is more important than outer appearance.
    - ○ **D.** They only liked the way butterflies look.

8. **"To really understand a person, you have to walk a mile in his or her shoes." What does that expression mean? Write your answer on a separate sheet of paper. Then write a paragraph about whose shoes you'd like to walk a mile in and how it might change your point of view.**

The Horrible Green Creature

A **Drawing Conclusions** Spooky Story

What happens to brothers and sisters who won't get along? Without giving away the story, let's just say it can be mighty scary. Beyond that you can draw your own conclusions. **Drawing conclusions** is putting together the information you have to make sense of what you're reading. Try it.

Johnny and Jennie were brother and sister, and they didn't get along. Johnny teased. Jennie bothered. Johnny bullied. Jennie whined.

"Stop it!" their mother would say.

"I didn't do anything," they would both answer.

On and on it went, never ending, never changing, always teasing and bothering, bullying and whining. Then one morning Johnny and Jennie's mother had to leave the two of them alone—together.

"Can you two stay alone for a few hours without causing trouble?" their mother asked.

"Oh, sure," Johnny replied.

"No problem," Jennie answered.

Within five minutes they were squabbling.

"I was first!" Jennie said.

"Get out of the way!" Johnny ordered.

"Go soak your head!" cried Jennie.

At that point, a horrible green creature came floating into the room. It had horrible scales, a horrible green head, horrible red eyes, horrible purple wings, and a ghastly grin that was so horrible that it gave you a stomachache.

"Who are you? What are you?" asked Jennie.

"I am a horrible green creature," replied the creature.

"Why are you here? What do you want from us?" Johnny asked.

"I'm sent to nasty situations—places where people are fighting for no good reason," the creature replied. "And this, for sure, is a nasty situation. I'm just here doing my job."

"Take a hike," said Johnny. "Get lost!"

"Wait," said Jennie. "What else do you do, horrible green creature?"

"Watch this," said the horrible green creature.

And with that, the creature took a deep breath, made a horrible face (even more horrible than its regular face), and blew a horrible cloud of hot green gas straight at the two kids.

POOSH!

"Yow!" cried Jennie. "That stings!"

"And it stinks, too," Johnny said. "Knock it off, would you creature?"

"Want me to knock it off? OK. I'll knock it off if the two of you will quit fighting," said the creature.

"Ask Jennie," said Johnny. "It's her fault."

"No way," said Jennie. "Talk to him."

"I'm not talking to anyone!" cried the creature.

And with that he started spraying stinky green gas clouds all over the room.

POOSH! POOSH! POOSH! POOSH!

"Stop!" both cried. "You're ruining our house. You'll get us in trouble."

"Good!" cried the horrible green creature. "I hope you two get in a lot of trouble."

"Hey," said Jennie, "that's a pretty nasty thing to say."

"Well, I'm a pretty nasty creature," said the creature.

"Hey, Jennie," said Johnny. "Will you help me get rid of this gasbag?"

---

1. What problem do Jennie and Johnny face?
- ○ **A.** They don't have anything to do.
- ○ **B.** They don't get along.
- ○ **C.** They don't listen to their mother.
- ○ **D.** They're afraid of ghosts.

2. Draw a conclusion about whose fault the problem is.
- ○ **A.** Johnny is mostly at fault.
- ○ **B.** Jennie is mostly at fault.
- ○ **C.** They're equally at fault.
- ○ **D.** All of the above are true.

3. The horrible green creature has probably come to Johnny and Jennie's house to
- ○ **A.** teach them how to cause problems.
- ○ **B.** teach them not to fight.
- ○ **C.** learn how to be horrible from them.
- ○ **D.** destroy things.

4. How do you think Johnny and Jennie will respond to the creature?
- ○ **A.** They will be so nasty that they will drive the creature away.
- ○ **B.** They will become friends with the creature.
- ○ **C.** They will call the police.
- ○ **D.** They will work together to get rid of the creature.

It was the first time he'd ever asked her to help him with anything.

"I sure will," Jennie said. "Let's work together."

And with that they went to the closet, grabbed the super-powerful vacuum cleaner that their mother used, and put it in reverse so it blew out instead of sucking in.

"Okay, creature," Johnny said. "We'll give you one chance. If you don't VAMOOSE right this instant, we're going to BLAST you with this reverse vacuum cleaner."

"You don't scare me!" cried the horrible green creature.

So while Johnny held the nozzle, Jennie pushed the button, and *BR-A-A-A-N-N-NG!* The machine started shooting at the creature.

"Yowsa!" cried the creature. "If there's one thing we horrible green creatures can't take, it's super-powered vacuums in reverse. I'm OUTTA HERE!"

And with that, the horrible green creature vanished as mysteriously as he'd arrived.

Jennie turned off the vacuum cleaner. The two dusted off their hands.

"Well, we sure took care of that," Johnny said.

"We sure did," Jennie replied.

At that moment their mother walked in.

"How did you two get along after I left?" she asked.

"Things were horrible at first," said Johnny. "Really horrible."

"But we worked together to make things better," Jennie said.

"Well, isn't that nice," said their mother.

"Yes, it is," said Jennie and Johnny.

And the two of them never acted horrible again. Well, almost never!

THE END

5. **Draw a conclusion about what Jennie and Johnny learned from their experience with the horrible green creature.**
   - ○ **A.** They learned that the creature was truly horrible.
   - ○ **B.** They learned that working together is very difficult.
   - ○ **C.** They learned that they could get along if they tried.
   - ○ **D.** They learned that their mother is never wrong.

6. **How did Jennie and Johnny's mother probably feel when she saw how well the two kids were getting along?**
   - ○ **A.** Unhappy
   - ○ **B.** Surprised
   - ○ **C.** Frightened
   - ○ **D.** Worried

7. **What seems to be the horrible green creature's job?**
   - ○ **A.** To frighten kids
   - ○ **B.** To baby-sit for bratty kids
   - ○ **C.** To help people stop fighting
   - ○ **D.** To punish brothers and sisters who fight

8. **Draw some conclusions about the horrible green creature's job. Imagine that you are the creature's boss. It's time for the creature to go out on his next job assignment. On a separate sheet of paper, write a memo (a paragraph) to the monster explaining the job. Describe who needs his help and why. Be creative!**

The House on Plum Street

An **Analyzing Plot** Spooky Story

Every story has characters, a setting, and some kind of action. All of these together is called the **plot**. Here, the plot focuses on a young man who will do anything—and we mean anything—to earn money for something he wants. The plot gets very creepy, very quickly. Check it out!

It started with greed. Some folks want money. Me? My name is Louis and I wanted a music system: A G-750 Blaster CD-Surround Total Theater System that costs $2,999.

How did I pay for it? In a word, I didn't. I put it on the installment plan. Each month, I paid $200— for 24 months.

This worked out OK, until I lost my job at the video store. Suddenly, I needed money, and I needed it fast. So when I saw the ad in the newspaper, I knew I had no choice. It read:

```
Make $100 a night.
Be the caretaker at
my great-great-uncle
Farley's house at
13 Plum Street, one
night a week. No
questions asked. Call
Jasper at LK5-1313.
```

I called and, just like the ad said, I got the job with no questions asked. Jasper handed me the key and promised me it would be an easy job, except for one thing: Some people said the house was haunted.

"Nonsense," I said. "I don't believe in haunted houses."

I will say this: The place was dark, dank, and full of cobwebs. The windows were cracked and broken. The floors creaked. Was it haunted?

Of course not, I told myself.

And for most of the night, there was no sign of anything strange. Then, the house's music system caught my eye. I had never seen one like it before. I turned it on. The most beautiful music came pouring out of unseen speakers. I'd never heard such music before. I couldn't identify the instruments or the style of music. I just knew it spoke directly to my heart, filling me with happiness and contentment. I looked at the label on the system. It was called a Bizarre-100.

I sat there and listened to the Bizarre-100 for most of the evening. I had no doubt that it was the greatest sound system in the world.

I decided that I had to have it.

1. **Who is the main character in the story?**
   - ○ **A.** Jasper
   - ○ **B.** Uncle Farley
   - ○ **C.** Louis
   - ○ **D.** The house

2. **What is the setting of the story?**
   - ○ **A.** A spooky old house
   - ○ **B.** A haunted music system
   - ○ **C.** The distant past
   - ○ **D.** Louis's apartment

3. **What problem does the main character face?**
   - ○ **A.** He doesn't have a music system.
   - ○ **B.** He doesn't have the money to pay for his music system.
   - ○ **C.** He needs to get his old job back from the video store.
   - ○ **D.** He is being pursued by a ghost.

4. **What steps does the main character take to solve the problem?**
   - ○ **A.** He decides to return the music system.
   - ○ **B.** He buys a very expensive music system.
   - ○ **C.** He tricks Uncle Jasper into giving him a new music system.
   - ○ **D.** He takes a job caring for a house that may be haunted.

I looked closely at the case. There was a small plaque that read: WHOSOEVER WANTS THIS SYSTEM, YOU CAN HAVE IT—IF YOU ARE TRULY WORTHY!

So the next morning, when I got ready to leave, I went over to the system. I tried to unplug it.

Suddenly, the room filled with a mournful, loathsome sound:

"You are not worthy! LEAVE ME ALO-O-ONE!"

A strange radio broadcast? Perhaps. When I tried to yank the plug out of the wall, it wouldn't budge. The terrible sound got louder:

"You are not worthy! LEAVE ME ALO-O-O-ONE!"

I gave it one more pull.

"You are truly not worthy! LEAVE ME ALO-O-O-O-ONE!"

At that point, the walls began to shake. The windows began to rattle. Cracks in the ceiling began to widen. Plaster began to fall.

I looked up. The ceiling was about to cave in!

I ran. I didn't turn around until I reached the front gate. Then I heard a terrible noise. The old house was collapsing!

I ran straight to Jasper and told him what happened.

"Finally," he said. "I've been waiting for Uncle Farley's house to fall apart for twenty years. You did it. You finally did it!"

"Tell me something," I said. "That music system in the house. Where did it come from? Was it your uncle's?"

"Music system?" Jasper replied. "That place didn't have a music system. It didn't even have a radio! My uncle moved out in 1912, before anyone in this town even had a radio."

Sure enough, when the workers came to clean up the wreckage, they found no sign of a sound system. And it should have survived the collapse.

Myself? I can't explain what happened. I still don't believe in haunted houses. Well, maybe a little bit.

One thing I definitely don't believe in is an expensive sound system. The day after the house collapsed, I traded in my $2,999 system for a plain old $129 set. And I like it fine. So taking the caretaking job did solve my problem—in a way. But sometimes, when I'm lying in bed at night, I close my eyes and think I hear the beautiful sounds that came from the Bizarre-100 system. I tell myself that somehow, somewhere, I'll hear that music again.

THE END

5. **In this section, what new problem does the main character face?**
   ○ **A.** He wants to play music, but the Bizarre-100 won't let him.
   ○ **B.** He wants to destroy the music system because he can't have it.
   ○ **C.** He wants to take the Bizarre-100 music system.
   ○ **D.** He wants to escape the house.

6. **What is the climax of the story?**
   ○ **A.** The house burns down when the music system overheats.
   ○ **B.** The house collapses when Louis tries to unplug the system.
   ○ **C.** The house is sold to Jasper for a small price.
   ○ **D.** Louis is attacked by a ghost.

7. **How does the main character change as a result of what happens in the story?**
   ○ **A.** He no longer believes in haunted houses.
   ○ **B.** He no longer likes music.
   ○ **C.** He is now a ghost.
   ○ **D.** He no longer wants a fancy, expensive sound system.

8. **You're a reporter for *The Haunted Times*, a magazine dedicated to tracking down ghosts and hauntings. On a separate sheet of paper, write an article describing what happened at Uncle Farley's house. Was it haunted—or not?**

The Hideous Blob's Amazing Comeback

A **Main Idea** and **Supporting Details** Spooky Story

The **main idea** is a story's big point. Often, you can figure out a story's main idea by asking yourself, "What is the main character's biggest problem?" **Supporting details** give you more information about the main idea. See how it works in this tale of a big blob who just isn't happy.

The Hideous Blob was a megastar. His last five movies—all horror movies, of course—had been smash hits. Fans adored him. Critics praised him. Everyone wanted a piece of him! The Blob was on magazine covers, TV shows, commercials, videos, you name it! He was America's favorite blob.

So was the Hideous Blob satisfied? Not a chance.

"I wish people would stop thinking of me as such a hideous blob," the Blob complained to his always-honest agent, Vickie Crackle.

"But you are a hideous blob—a gob of oozing goo," the ever-honest Vickie said. "And on top of that, you're nice!"

"But I want to stretch myself," the Blob said to Vickie. "I've been typecast. I know I can move into other roles. I don't want to be stuck playing blobs for the rest of my life."

"What kinds of roles were you thinking of?" asked Vickie.

"In my next movie," the Blob said, "I would like to play an action hero. Something like Harrison Ford would have done in his younger days—*Star Wars, Raiders of the Lost Ark*, that sort of thing.

"OK! I'm on top of it, Blob!" said Vickie. "But I have to be honest. I'm not sure it's a great idea."

1. What is the main idea so far?
- ○ **A.** The Blob wants to be famous.
- ○ **B.** The Blob wants to try new roles.
- ○ **C.** The Blob wants to make commercials and TV shows.
- ○ **D.** The Blob wants to quit acting and start a singing career.

2. Which detail supports the idea that the Blob is a big star?
- ○ **A.** The Blob has an agent named Vickie Crackle.
- ○ **B.** The Blob appears on magazine covers.
- ○ **C.** The Blob is not satisfied with his career.
- ○ **D.** The Blob likes Harrison Ford.

3. Which detail supports the idea that Vickie is always honest?
- ○ **A.** Vickie says, "That may not be such a great idea."
- ○ **B.** Vickie never takes any money from the Blob.
- ○ **C.** Vickie says, "You are the best Blob in the entire world."
- ○ **D.** Vickie says, "I'm on top of it."

In the Blob's next movie, fans got to see their favorite star drive a souped-up sports car, battle evil ninjas, and win the heart of a beautiful woman. Did they like the new him?

Not a chance. People hated the Blob's new movie.

"Ick!" they said.

"Disgusting!" they cried.

"I wish he'd go back to being the old Hideous Blob that we knew and loved," they said.

"The Blob is simply not believable as an action hero," wrote a famous movie critic. "The Blob is a blob, and that's all there is to it."

But the Blob didn't go back to being the old Hideous Blob. In fact, he made several more movies in which he got to "stretch" himself. In one, he was a romantic but emotionally damaged

math genius. In another he played a guy with glasses who was a meek newspaper reporter by day and a crime-fighting hero by night. They were complete flops as well.

Before, people stood in line to see the Blob's movies. Now, theaters showing his films were practically empty.

Finally, the Blob came to Vickie. "You've got to do something," he said. "You've got to help me become popular again!"

"OK," Vickie said, "but it's going to mean going back to horror movies."

"That's fine," said the Blob. "I understand now. I'm a great horror-movie actor, but I'm a terrible action hero."

"I have to say I agree with you," said Vickie. "But at least you gave it an honest try. It would have bothered you all your life if you hadn't!"

"And I have to admit it," said the Blob. "I always felt ridiculous in those cool-guy outfits."

So Vickie had the Hideous Blob make a new scary movie in which he was the old Hideous Blob again. Audiences loved it.

"This is great!" they cried.

"The Hideous Blob for president!" they shouted.

And so it went. The Hideous Blob became a big star again. He was on commercials, TV shows, and in magazines. And he got awards—Blob of the Year, Best Supporting Blob, even Comeback Blob of the Year.

Of course, the Blob gave tons of interviews. In each one, he took the opportunity to put in a plug for his new message: "Be happy with who you are." The Blob wasn't an action hero. But now, he was a different kind of hero. He was a hero to unusual people everywhere. And that was an exciting new role for him. **THE END**

4. **What detail shows that audiences did not like the Blob in his new roles?**
   - ○ **A.** A critic said the Blob should stick to horror movies.
   - ○ **B.** Vickie said she thought the Blob's plan to take new roles wasn't a good idea.
   - ○ **C.** The Blob took a role as a crime-fighting reporter.
   - ○ **D.** Theaters showing his films were nearly empty.

5. **Audiences didn't like the new Blob because**
   - ○ **A.** he wasn't believable.
   - ○ **B.** he lost his acting ability.
   - ○ **C.** he was too scary.
   - ○ **D.** he said nasty things about his fans.

6. **The Blob asked Vickie to help him**
   - ○ **A.** convince critics he was good in his new roles.
   - ○ **B.** play a blob again.
   - ○ **C.** get revenge on people who didn't like the new him.
   - ○ **D.** spread his new message.

7. **At first, the Blob dreamed of becoming an action hero. Instead he became a hero to people who are**
   - ○ **A.** scared.
   - ○ **B.** overweight.
   - ○ **C.** different.
   - ○ **D.** sick.

8. **You are a writer for *Scary Teen Movie* magazine. On a separate sheet of paper, write a short article about the Blob's big comeback and his new mission in life.**

The Butcher and His Wife

A **Making Inferences** Spooky Story

When something creepy is going on, you want to get to the bottom of it. At times like those, inference really comes in handy. An **inference** is like an educated guess. When you use clues from a story to figure out things that the author doesn't tell you, you're making inferences. Try it in this one-of-a-kind ghost story.

Aunt Elizabeth had always been Sara's favorite aunt. So when Aunt Liz had a problem, Sara didn't hesitate to come and help. Aunt Liz had recently moved to a faraway town and bought a big old house. It was only after Sara arrived on the train that Aunt Liz told her what the real trouble was: The old house she'd bought seemed to have ghosts.

"Did you say g-ghosts?" Sara gulped.

"Yes," Aunt Liz said calmly. "And I need you to help me get rid of them."

"G-get rid of them," Sara repeated. "H-how?"

In a steady voice, Aunt Liz explained. There were two ghosts: Morgan the Butcher and his wife Cynthia. Each night when it got dark, in a ghostly, moaning voice, the Butcher and his wife would appear and ask the same question: "WHAT DOES MORGAN

THE BUTCHER WEIGH?"

Then they would cackle madly into the dark night.

"What a strange question," Sara said to Aunt Liz. "Is that all the ghosts ever say?"

"Yes," answered Aunt Liz. "Over and over again, they ask the same question. And they never stop laughing. It's puzzling, isn't it? But I know that if we can find the answer to the question, we can get rid of the ghosts."

Sara was determined to solve the puzzle. At the local library she researched the topic of ghosts and tried to track down information about what Morgan the Butcher and Cynthia had been like when they were alive.

What she found puzzled her. Most ghosts lived unhappy lives. But Morgan and Cynthia seemed to have been happy—and popular, too. Everyone seemed to love to come to their little shop and buy sausages and hear the jokes that they told. Both Morgan and Cynthia were renowned jokers.

But as far as answering the question, "WHAT DOES MORGAN THE BUTCHER WEIGH?" Sara could only guess.

"One hundred fifty pounds?" she said, in response to the ghosts' question.

"NO-O-O!" the ghosts cackled.

"One hundred sixty pounds?" she asked.

"NO, NO, NO!" the ghosts moaned.

It went on like this. Then one night Sara had an idea: Morgan was a ghost, and ghosts were weightless spirits. So when they asked, "WHAT DOES MORGAN WEIGH?" Sara answered, "Nothing." He didn't weigh anything at all.

But this made them cackle and moan more than ever.

"NO, NO, NO, NO, NO, NO, NO!" they shrieked.

Sara kept trying different answers for the ghosts. But finally the day came when she had to leave. That night, Sara had a ticket to go back home on the midnight train.

1. **Make an inference about the relationship between Sara and Aunt Liz.**
   - ○ **A.** Aunt Liz was the coach of Sara's soccer team.
   - ○ **B.** Aunt Liz and Sara once lived near each other and were close.
   - ○ **C.** Aunt Liz and Sara once lived in a haunted house together in a different town.
   - ○ **D.** Aunt Liz and Sara had always lived far apart but stayed in touch on the phone.

2. **What helped you make your inference for question 1?**
   - ○ **A.** It says Aunt Liz "recently moved to a faraway town."
   - ○ **B.** It says Aunt Liz had recently "bought a big old house."
   - ○ **C.** It says "the old house that she'd bought seemed to have ghosts."
   - ○ **D.** The fact that one of the ghosts was a butcher.

3. **Make an inference about Aunt Liz's attitude toward ghosts.**
   - ○ **A.** She is so terrified them.
   - ○ **B.** She enjoys them and finds them amusing.
   - ○ **C.** She does not believe in them.
   - ○ **D.** They bother her but she is not overly afraid of them.

4. **What helped you make your inference for question 3?**
   - ○ **A.** Aunt Liz spoke in a nervous voice.
   - ○ **B.** Aunt Liz spoke in a calm and steady voice.
   - ○ **C.** Aunt Liz spoke in a loud voice.
   - ○ **D.** Aunt Liz called Sara for help.

"I'm sorry," she told her Aunt Liz. "I wish I could've been more help."

"That's all right," Aunt Liz said. "You tried. Come on. I'll walk you to your train."

On the way to the train station they passed by the little sausage shop that had once belonged to Morgan the Butcher. Inside, Sara saw a man weighing out sausages.

"Wait a second!" Sara suddenly cried. "I think I know the answer to the ghosts' question. Let's go back to the house one more time, Aunt Liz."

"But you'll miss your train," Aunt Liz said.

"That's okay," Sara said. "Let's go. Quickly. Before we miss everything!"

They arrived at the house just in time. The ghosts were in fine form, shrieking all over the house:

"WHAT DOES MORGAN THE BUTCHER WEIGH?"

But this time, Sara knew the answer to their question.

"Sausages!" she cried.

The ghosts suddenly stopped.

"What did you say?" they asked in their ghostly, moaning voices.

"I said, Morgan the Butcher weighs SAUSAGES!" Sara cried.

This did it. Once the laughter started, it sounded like it would never stop. Louder and louder it got, a rip-snorting, bone-rattling guffaw.

"HA HA HO HO HEE HEE HAR HAR HO HO HA HA!"

The ghosts sounded like they would never stop laughing.

It was the one final joke that Morgan the Butcher and his wife Cynthia wanted to tell the world:

WHAT DOES MORGAN THE BUTCHER WEIGH?

HE WEIGHS SAUSAGES!

Get it? It was pretty funny. In fact, it was so funny that the ghosts never came back again.

THE END

---

5. **What did Sara see that helped her figure out the answer to the riddle?**
   - ○ **A.** A butcher weighing sausages on a scale
   - ○ **B.** The location of the butcher shop
   - ○ **C.** Her Aunt Liz eating sausage
   - ○ **D.** A chapter in a library book

6. **The answer to the ghosts' question turned out to be a joke. What helped Sarah infer that the ghosts were joking?**
   - ○ **A.** Knowing that Morgan was an extremely happy man
   - ○ **B.** Knowing that Cynthia and Morgan were famous for their senses of humor
   - ○ **C.** Knowing that Cynthia and Morgan cheated their customers
   - ○ **D.** Reading about joking ghosts in the library

7. **Make an inference about ghosts based on this story.**
   - ○ **A.** They can have a good sense of humor.
   - ○ **B.** They can have a job as a butcher.
   - ○ **C.** They live only in dark old houses.
   - ○ **D.** They are rude.

8. **Write a thank-you note that Morgan and Cynthia might write to Aunt Liz and Sara, thanking them for getting their joke—and allowing them to take a rest from haunting.**

The Three Ghosts of Lucy Bly

An **Understanding Character** Spooky Story

Good **characters** make stories interesting to read. It's fun to figure out what makes a character tick. Ask yourself, "What's going on in the character's head?" or "Why would the character do such a stupid thing?" Try it in this story of a not-so-nice girl who gets what she deserves.

"**L**ucy Bly, you're a total traitor," said Francy-Jean Swain, Lucy's best friend. Lucy and Francy-Jean were supposed to go to a concert together. But then two girls from their school's super-cool crowd, Molly and Polly, called. They asked Lucy to come to their slumber party. Lucy decided to go.

Lucy was in her room, sitting on her bed, listening to Z-105, her favorite radio station. The slumber party wouldn't begin for two hours. Lucy knew that as her best friend, Francy-Jean must have been disappointed and perhaps a bit furious. But what could Lucy do? Molly and Polly were just about the most popular girls at Webster Middle School! How could Lucy say no to them?

"I couldn't," she told herself. And if Francy-Jean didn't understand that, well, that was her problem!

1. **From what you have read so far, which word best describes Lucy's character?**
   - A. Disloyal
   - B. Loyal
   - C. Mean
   - D. Kind

2. **What actions support this view of Lucy's character?**
   - A. She does nothing but sit in her room and listen to the radio.
   - B. She decides to go to the concert rather than the slumber party.
   - C. She decides to go to the slumber party rather than the concert.
   - D. She breaks a promise to go out with her best friend.

3. **How does Lucy justify her actions to herself?**
   - A. She says that Francy-Jean doesn't understand how to be a friend.
   - B. She says that she can't say no to the popular girls.
   - C. She says that she can't say no to Francy-Jean.
   - D. She says Francy-Jean won't mind going to the concert alone.

4. **Which of these sentences from the story shows that, deep down, Lucy knows that what she did was wrong?**
   - A. If Francy-Jean didn't understand that, well, that was her problem!
   - B. Lucy knew that as her best friend, Francy-Jean must have been disappointed.
   - C. Lucy and Francy-Jean were supposed to go to a concert together.
   - D. Molly and Polly were just about the most popular girls at Webster Middle School!

he radio kept playing. And Lucy grew more and more sleepy. Soon, she dozed off. Some time later, she was awakened by a strange light glowing in her room.

"LUCY!" called a horrible, squealing, weasel-like voice. "LUCY BLY, DO YOU HEAR ME?"

Lucy sat up like a bolt. "Who's that?" she cried.

"I AM THE WEASEL-GHOST OF FRIENDSHIPS PAST," replied the voice.

"Why are you a weasel?" Lucy asked.

"Because, like a weasel, you abandoned your past friendships," said the voice. "Do you remember Wendy Gerber, Dara Diaz, and Lannie Plansky?"

"Of course," Lucy said. "Those are the names of my best friends. My former best friends."

"Just like a weasel, you dumped them all," the voice said. "Why, Lucy? Why were you such a weasel?"

"I don't know," said Lucy. "But I've had enough of this—this dream or whatever it is. I'm waking up now."

And with that, Lucy shook her head, and the weasel-ghost was gone.

"Whew!" Lucy said. "What a bad dream. That's enough of that." But a few moments later, another strange light appeared, and another ghost entered the room.

"I AM THE SNAKE-GHOST OF FRIENDSHIPS PRESENT," hissed the hideous figure. "I take the form of a snake to show the low, treacherous way in which you treat your current friends. I am speaking of Francy-Jean Swain. Why did you betray her, Lucy? Why?"

"I don't know," Lucy said.

Like a hideous rope, the snake-ghost writhed and coiled, twisting around itself as it hissed and moaned.

"This is ridiculous!" cried Lucy. And she grabbed a broom and whisked the ghost out of the room. But it wasn't long before a third ghost appeared.

"I AM THE GHOST OF FUTURE FRIENDSHIPS," said the ghost.

"Why can't I see you?" Lucy asked.

"Because there is nothing to see," said the voice. "In the future, you won't have any friends."

"That's ridiculous," said Lucy. "I'll always have friends. If not Francy-Jean, then Molly and Polly."

"Are you sure?" asked the ghost.

And then, two horrible figures appeared in the room. They looked like pigs. Yet, at the same time, they had the faces of Molly and Polly.

"Oink, oink, Lucy!" the pig-ghosts teased. "We're the most popular girls in school. Will YOU be our friend? Oink oink!"

"Y-A-A-A-H!" Lucy screamed.

This was too much.

Lucy sat up ramrod straight on her bed. The strange lights were gone. The pig-ghosts were gone. The radio was still tuned to Z-105. Hardly any time had passed since Lucy had fallen asleep.

"I was asleep, wasn't I?" said Lucy to herself.

She had a sudden urge to call Francy-Jean on the phone. "Francy-Jean," she said, when her friend answered. "I've been thinking. Is it still possible to go to the concert with you?"

"What happened?" Francy-Jean said. "Did you get ditched by Molly and Polly?"

"No," Lucy said. "Actually, you could say that I ditched them. I decided I'd rather hang out with you tonight."

"Sure you don't want to change your mind?" Francy-Jean asked.

"There's not a ghost of a chance," Lucy said. And she meant it.

THE END

5. **Taken all together, what do Lucy's dreams reveal?**
   - ○ **A.** Deep down inside, she knows she needs to be loyal to her true friends.
   - ○ **B.** Deep down inside, she knows she needs to be loyal to the most popular kids.
   - ○ **C.** Deep down inside, she knows she needs to pretend to be loyal to her friends.
   - ○ **D.** Deep down inside, she knows that friends are unimportant.

6. **When Lucy says she changed her mind and wants to go to the concert, Francy-Jean asks, "Did you get ditched by Molly and Polly?" This shows that**
   - ○ **A.** Francy-Jean didn't mind that Lucy dropped her for Molly and Polly.
   - ○ **B.** Francy-Jean isn't her friend anymore.
   - ○ **C.** Francy-Jean is going to the slumber party.
   - ○ **D.** Francy-Jean doesn't totally trust Lucy.

7. **How does Lucy change as a result of her dreams?**
   - ○ **A.** She tries to become a more loyal friend.
   - ○ **B.** She becomes less loyal to Molly and Polly.
   - ○ **C.** She becomes more of a loner.
   - ○ **D.** She tries to focus more on her schoolwork.

8. **Imagine that you're Lucy. On a separate sheet of paper, write an apology note to Francy-Jean. Explain how you have changed.**

Ask Aunt Doty:

An Advice Column for the Supernaturally Inclined

An **Author's Purpose** Spooky Story

Authors write for a reason. That reason is called an **author's purpose**. Most science-book authors write to teach. That's their main purpose. Ghost-story authors usually have two purposes: to scare and to entertain. Old Aunt Doty is a columnist for the *Creeptown Daily News*. What's her purpose for writing? Who are her readers?

```
Dear Aunt Doty,
   I'm going to my aunt's 375th
birthday party next week. What would
be a good gift for someone who likes
a good time?
         — Gasgack, the Evil One
```

Dear Gas,

Great big gobs of murkalated monkey-meat are always a fine gift for a fun-loving relative. But if you can't swing that, try a big bag of scorpions. They're handy, fun, and just poisonous enough to liven up any occasion. Put a couple in somebody's shoe and watch the fun begin!

Yours truly,
Aunt Doty

```
Dear Aunt Doty,
   I can't stand my boss at my after-
school job and I'd like to give him
the Evil Eye. What's correct—to give
the Evil Eye first and then spit? Or
should I spit first?
         — Spittin' Jim
```

Dear Jim,

   Either way is good. As long as you truly wish the worst, you can't go wrong. Or should I say—you can't go right!

                    Yours truly,
                    Aunt Doty

Dear Aunt Doty,

   I came into work the other day, and my coworkers dumped a bucket of fish guts over my head. The smell was heavenly! What can I get to thank them?
                    — Something Fishy
                         in Reading

Dear Fish,

   I have one word that will solve your problem perfectly: bedbugs. Have them professionally installed. It's the gift that keeps on giving—or should I say biting!

                    Yours truly,
                    Aunt Doty

1. **Which word in the title gives you the best clue to Aunt Doty's purpose?**
   ○ **A.** Dear
   ○ **B.** Inclined
   ○ **C.** Column
   ○ **D.** Advice

2. **Which do you most strongly agree with? The author wants to**
   ○ **A.** give information.
   ○ **B.** gather information.
   ○ **C.** make a request.
   ○ **D.** frighten.

3. **Authors can have more than one purpose. In this case, the author seems to be trying to**
   ○ **A.** apologize and persuade the audience.
   ○ **B.** persuade and scare the audience.
   ○ **C.** entertain and inform the audience.
   ○ **D.** apologize and scare the audience.

4. **The purpose of the people who write to Aunt Doty is to**
   ○ **A.** inform Aunt Doty.
   ○ **B.** ask for help from Aunt Doty.
   ○ **C.** entertain Aunt Doty.
   ○ **D.** scare Aunt Doty.

Dear Aunt Doty,

   Last week, I cast a spell on our mailman and turned him into a chicken. Now I'm having second thoughts. What should I do?
                    — Hope I'm Not
                         Chickening Out

Dear Hope,

   It's quite natural to feel this way after you turn a mailman into a chicken. But don't worry, you'll get used to it—though he might not! Cluck cluck!

                    Yours truly,
                    Aunt Doty

Dear Aunt Doty,

Last Halloween, my two best friends got together and infested my house with mice and vampire bats. It's so cool! What can I do for them to show that I care?

— Stumped in Pittsburgh

Dear Stump,

Why don't you try filling their lockers at school with buckets of fresh green slime mold? To find sources for excellent mold, go to my Web site, <u>AuntDoty.aargh</u> and click on "Repulsive Ideas." You'll find all kinds of creative ways to gross out your loved ones.

Yours truly,
Aunt Doty

Dear Aunt Doty,

My room is really dull. How can I spruce it up?

— Dullsville

Dear Dull,

Fresh roadkill always hits the spot. It's colorful, yet it's always in perfect taste. And the bonus is, it starts to smell after a while.

Yours truly,
Aunt Doty

5. In real life, a person whose house was infested with bats and mice would be angry. But the person who wrote the letter at left was happy. Her purpose for writing to Aunt Doty was to get ideas for ways to _____ the people who had done it.
   ○ **A.** hurt
   ○ **B.** punish
   ○ **C.** scare
   ○ **D.** thank

6. Aunt Doty is writing for a certain kind of reader. Which of the following best describes her audience?
   ○ **A.** Animal lovers
   ○ **B.** Athletes
   ○ **C.** Teenage musicians
   ○ **D.** Creepy beings

7. If a girl wrote to Aunt Doty asking what to wear to the prom, which of the following answers would Aunt Doty probably give?
   ○ **A.** A simple black dress and a string of pearls
   ○ **B.** A frilly gown and high-heeled pumps
   ○ **C.** Jeans and a ripped T-shirt
   ○ **D.** A slime-soaked dress and spiderweb cape

8. Imagine that you're a resident of Creeptown. On a separate sheet of paper, write your own letter to Aunt Doty. Pair up with a classmate and answer each others' letters. Have fun!

The Choice

A **Making Predictions** Spooky Story

When you're watching a movie, do you guess what's going to happen next? If so, you're **making a prediction**. When you read, you can do the same thing. Try it here. Use the clues in the story plus your own common sense.

Old Henry Hasperson was getting on in years, and he decided it was time to hand out some of his large fortune. He had two living relatives: a nephew, Steve, and a niece, Janet. One Saturday afternoon he invited them to his mansion.

"I have decided to let you choose your own inheritance," he told them. "As long as your choice is honest, you will get the reward you deserve."

"What are our choices?" asked Janet.

"There are only two things I can give you," Uncle Henry said. "You can choose my money or you can choose my Three Pillars of Wisdom."

"Your Three Pillars of Wisdom?" asked Janet.

"That's right," said Uncle Henry. "In my long life I have learned that only three things are absolutely true. I call them my Three Pillars of Wisdom."

Janet knew that wisdom was a very valuable thing. But unlike her cousin Steve, whose family had tons of money, she had grown up poor. Not only was Steve rich, he didn't even seem interested in money. It didn't seem to mean anything to him. He drove an old car and wore nothing but faded jeans and worn T-shirts.

But money meant a great deal to Janet. Could she afford to make a mistake? And what exactly did Uncle Henry mean by an "honest choice"? Janet was surprised to hear him talking about honesty anyway. It was common knowledge in the family that he'd made much of his money by tricking and cheating his competitors.

"What if we choose the wrong thing?" Janet asked.

"You will receive only the reward that you deserve," Uncle Henry repeated. He gave each of them one day to make up their minds.

1. **What fact makes it seem likely that Janet will choose the money?**
   - ○ **A.** Uncle Henry has lots of money.
   - ○ **B.** Steve comes from a rich family.
   - ○ **C.** Janet knows wisdom is important.
   - ○ **D.** Janet comes from a poor family.

2. **Is it possible to predict for certain what choice Janet or Steve will make?**
   - ○ **A.** Yes
   - ○ **B.** No

3. **What fact makes it seem likely that Steve will choose the Three Pillars of Wisdom?**
   - ○ **A.** He is very interested in wisdom.
   - ○ **B.** He announced that will be his choice.
   - ○ **C.** He is rich and seems uninterested in money.
   - ○ **D.** He comes from a poor family.

4. **What fact makes it seem possible that Uncle Henry has some kind of trick up his sleeve?**
   - ○ **A.** He said he was planning a big trick.
   - ○ **B.** He is old.
   - ○ **C.** He often cheated in business.
   - ○ **D.** He has a reputation for being strange.

"This isn't fair," Janet complained, as she and Steve were walking home. "How are we supposed to make a choice?"

"Just tell the truth," Steve said. "Tell him you want the money. He'll give it to you."

"No, he won't," Janet said. "He'll think I'm greedy and he'll give the money to you. And you don't even want the money, do you, Steve?"

Steve shrugged. "I'll tell you what," he said. "Why don't I say that I want the money? He'll know I'm not being honest. So he'll end up giving it to you."

"Hmm," said Janet. "That's pretty clever. Would you do that for me?"

"Hey," Steve said. "We're not just cousins. We're friends. What are friends for?"

Janet was amazed. Though she and Steve had known each other for years, they'd never been especially close. Nor had she ever known Steve to be so generous.

"And anyway," Steve added, "if he does give me the money, we'll just split it. So either way you win."

"Wow!" said Janet. This was too good to be true.

5. **What new fact now makes it seem likely that Janet will choose the Pillars?**
   - ○ **A.** Steve has a plan to get Uncle Henry to give Janet the money.
   - ○ **B.** She has a new interest in wisdom.
   - ○ **C.** She no longer needs money.
   - ○ **D.** Uncle Henry told her to choose the Pillars.

6. **What is one thing that could go wrong for Janet if she follows Steve's plan?**
   - ○ **A.** Uncle Henry could lose all his money.
   - ○ **B.** Janet could wind up with too much wisdom.
   - ○ **C.** Another cousin could turn up and ask for the money.
   - ○ **D.** Steve could take the money and refuse to give Janet any.

7. **If Janet honestly chooses to receive the Three Pillars of Wisdom instead of the money, what would it show about her beliefs?**
   - ○ **A.** She believes that money can solve all problems.
   - ○ **B.** She believes wisdom is worth a lot of money.
   - ○ **C.** She believes in ghosts.
   - ○ **D.** She believes money isn't the most important thing in life.

Janet decided to go along with the plan. Steve would see Uncle Henry first. When he was done, Steve would wait outside for Janet in a white limo.

"A white limo?" Janet asked.

"You bet," said Steve. "Tomorrow, I'm hiring a white limo to take us home after we see Uncle Henry. To celebrate. No more walking for these cousins!"

The next day, things started out smoothly. The two arrived at Uncle Henry's mansion. The white limo waited outside. Steve went in to see Uncle Henry first. When he came out, he was holding a million-dollar check in his hand. He gave Janet the thumbs-up sign.

"I'll be waiting for you," Steve told her. He went out to wait in the white limo while Janet went in to see Uncle Henry.

"You are my favorite niece," Uncle Henry said to Janet. "What would you like to inherit from me?"

"Your Three Pillars of Wisdom, Uncle Henry," Janet said.

A strange smile spread across Uncle Henry's face. "The first pillar is rather simple," he said. "Honesty is for fools."

Janet was shocked. "Honesty is for fools!" she cried. "What kind of wisdom is that?"

"The kind of wisdom that made me millions!" Uncle Henry laughed.

"And your second pillar?" Janet asked.

"Never trust anyone!" Uncle Henry said.

Here, Janet knew that Uncle Henry was wrong.

"You have to have trust," she told him. "Trust is everything."

"Ha!" laughed Uncle Henry. "You seemed to have trusted your cousin Steve, and there he goes!"

Janet ran to the window. It couldn't be. But it was true. Steve had betrayed her. There was the white limo with Steve inside, pulling away! She was being left behind!

"Don't you want to hear what my third pillar of wisdom is?" Uncle Henry asked.

"Why not?" said Janet. Everything was ruined. Steve was gone. The money was gone. So why not collect a bit of Uncle Henry's heartless wisdom before she left for good?

"Everyone gets what they deserve," Uncle Henry said.

It was a cruel joke. But it seemed less cruel after Uncle Henry handed Janet a piece of paper.

"What's this?" she asked.

"A check for one million dollars," Uncle Henry said.

"But what about Steve?" Janet cried.

"Oh, he got a check, too," Uncle Henry said. "But unfortunately for Steve, his check was made out to a fake account. When he tries to cash it he'll find out it's worthless."

"And me?" Janet asked.

"You got what you deserved," Uncle Henry said. "It's as simple as that."

THE END

---

8. Imagine that Steve and Janet meet up exactly one year later. Using your imagination and evidence from the story, make a prediction about what the meeting would be like. On a separate sheet of paper, write the conversation they might have.

A Really Bad Hair Day

A **Reading for Details** Spooky Story

Details are the little things that, added together, make a story real. They make it scary, funny, or sad. Details help you understand the twists and turns of the plot and the changes the characters go through. As you read this story, pay careful attention to the details—if you dare.

Peter, Flora, and Ralph were sitting around talking about bad hair days.

"I have the worst bad hair days," Peter complained. "Some mornings I wake up and look like I've had my finger in an electric socket all night."

"No, I have the worst hair days," said Flora.

"You think you have bad hair days?" Ralph retorted. "I can top them all!"

"Oh, yeah?" Peter said. "This I've got to hear."

"I was at the mall," Ralph began. "I walked by this little hair shop called Maggs. A man sticks his head out and says, 'Bad hair day? No problem. I'll give you a haircut for free!'"

"So what did you do?" Flora asked.

"Are you kidding?" Ralph said. "I'd never turn down a free haircut."

"So how was it?" said Flora.

"The haircut?" Ralph said. "Fine. But when Maggs finished, he handed me a jar of what he called his Magic Gel. 'It'll do miracles for your hair,' he says. 'Only $39.95.'"

"Did you buy it?" asked Peter.

"No way," said Ralph. "I told him I wasn't interested. But he wouldn't let me leave. He goes, 'What? I give you a free haircut and you won't pay for a lousy jar of gel!'"

"That's not fair!" said Flora.

"'I know!" said Ralph. "We argued, but I didn't give in. I didn't pay him a cent for the haircut . . . or the gel.

"So he says, 'Watch out, you may be having a bad hair day after all.'"

Peter raised his eyebrows. "So, what did he mean—a bad hair day?"

---

1. **The story begins with a discussion among friends about which of them has had a worse**
   - ○ **A.** haircut.
   - ○ **B.** hair day.
   - ○ **C.** birthday.
   - ○ **D.** toothache.

2. **Who is the main character in the story so far?**
   - ○ **A.** Peter
   - ○ **B.** Flora
   - ○ **C.** Ralph
   - ○ **D.** There is no main character.

3. **In the story, Ralph is describing something that happened to**
   - ○ **A.** his father.
   - ○ **B.** Peter.
   - ○ **C.** a hairstylist.
   - ○ **D.** Ralph.

4. **Was the haircut really free?**
   - ○ **A.** Yes, it was free, but Ralph had to pay for a comb.
   - ○ **B.** No, it was not free because Ralph had to pay tax.
   - ○ **C.** Yes, it was free but Ralph was then offered a jar of expensive hair gel.
   - ○ **D.** No, it cost $39.95.

"So then what?" Flora asked.

"I'm walking through the mall," Ralph said. "I pass this big mean-looking guy with tattoos and a motorcycle helmet. Then I hear this tiny voice coming from somewhere that says: 'You big jerk!'"

"Who was it?" Flora asked.

"I don't know," said Ralph. "The tattoo guy turns to me and says, 'What'd you call me?' and I said, 'Nothing. I didn't say a word.'

"Then the tiny voice says again to him: 'Jerk!' So now the tattoo guy's angry," said Ralph. "He reaches out to grab me, but I run. It wasn't until I reached the other side of the mall that I realized where the voice was coming from: MY OWN HAIR!"

"Your hair?" said Flora. "Your hair was *talking*?"

"And that's not all," Ralph continued. "When I finally get away from the mean tattoo guy, a security guard from Tempo's comes up to me. He accuses me of shoplifting."

"You're kidding!" gasped Flora.

"I said, 'Shoplifting! What are you talking about?'" said Ralph. "Then the security guard reaches into my hair and pulls out a pair of diamond cuff links from Tempo's."

"Your *hair* stole the cuff links?" Peter asked.

"I guess so," Ralph replied. "I sure didn't steal them."

"This is unreal," exclaimed Flora. "Then what happened?"

Ralph continued. "While I'm running from the security guard—I don't know how this happened, but my hair reaches out and knocks over a ladder, which crashes through the window of a bookstore and knocks over a huge display of books. A guy from the bookstore called out to me: 'You come back here!'"

"Wow," said Flora. "Are you kidding me?"

"So by now," Ralph said, "I'm being chased by the cuff-link guy and the bookstore guy, when who do I run into—the mean tattoo guy! He calls out to me, 'Get back here, you little weasel!'"

"My goodness," said Flora. "So what did you do?"

"They were closing in on me," said Ralph, "when suddenly, in the distance, I see Maggs the haircutter motioning me back into his shop. I run in there."

"He wanted to help you?" asked Peter.

"No!" said Ralph. "Maggs says, 'Now do you want to buy my Magic Gel?' I go, 'You bet, here's the money.'"

"You're joking," said Peter.

"Cross my heart and hope to spit," Ralph said.

"Then what?" Flora asked.

"For some reason, the security guard, bookstore guy, and mean tattoo guy don't follow me into Maggs's shop," Ralph said. "I don't know why. Anyway, when I come out, they were gone. Completely disappeared. So I went home."

"Wow," said Peter. "That's some real bad hair day!"

"You sure did beat us!" cried Flora. "By the way, what ever happened to the Magic Gel?"

"I rub a little bit of it in my hair every morning," Ralph said. "The jar never seems to run out. And I never have a bad hair day!"

THE END

---

5. **What seemed to be causing Ralph's problems?**
   - ○ **A.** His cuff links
   - ○ **B.** His hair
   - ○ **C.** Flora and Peter
   - ○ **D.** Bad luck

6. **How did Ralph change his mind at the end of the story?**
   - ○ **A.** He decided to get a haircut after all.
   - ○ **B.** He decided to buy some cuff links.
   - ○ **C.** He decided to buy the hair gel after all.
   - ○ **D.** He decided he didn't like the haircut after all.

7. **What happened to the people who were chasing Ralph?**
   - ○ **A.** They turned friendly.
   - ○ **B.** They apologized.
   - ○ **C.** They vowed to get back at him.
   - ○ **D.** They seemed to disappear.

8. **Have you ever had a bad hair day or a terrible haircut, or have you known someone who has? On a separate sheet of paper, write a paragraph describing it. Try to be funny (but not mean!) and use as many descriptive words as you can.**

Ratkins!

An **Understanding Setting** Spooky Story

A story's **setting** is where and when the story takes place. Some stories have just one setting; the story begins and ends in a single place, like the dungeon of a creepy castle in the year 1423. But in most stories the setting shifts from place to place. In the story you're about to read, one of the settings is truly out of this world.

It was a big night for Billie Bloom. She and her friend Baxter strolled into Shortie's Back Room and looked around. For years, Billie and Baxter had dreamed of being professional singers. Finally, all their hard work had paid off.

Shortie's, a trendy and popular club in their hometown of Strangeville, had hired them to sing their jazzy duets. Shortie's couldn't pay much. But it was a job. More than a job—it was a dream come true.

Billie and Baxter strode onto the small stage at Shortie's. Billie gazed out at the audience of patrons dressed in casual but stylish outfits. Candles flickered on the tables. As Billie began the first set, her heart filled with happiness.

That night, after she and Baxter finished their show, Billie was relaxing in her dressing room. There was a knock at the door. "Come in!" called Billie. In walked a small, rat-faced man chomping on a fat cigar. He handed her his card. It said, "B. Craven, President, RODENT ENTERTAINMENT."

"I heard you in there," Mr. Craven said to Billie. "You've got talent. You're too good for Shortie's Back Room."

"I am?" Billie said.

"I can make you a star," said Mr. Craven.

"You can?" asked Billie.

There were only two conditions: First, Billie would need to sign a contract with Mr. Craven. And second, she needed to get rid of Baxter.

"But Baxter and I are partners!" Billie said. "We've been planning this together for years."

"Look," Mr. Craven said. "Do you want to be somebody's partner . . . or a star? You decide."

---

1. **What is the setting as the story begins?**
   - ○ **A.** Shortie's Back Room
   - ○ **B.** Billie's house
   - ○ **C.** Baxter's house
   - ○ **D.** The offices of Rodent Entertainment

2. **Which time period seems accurate for this story?**
   - ○ **A.** 100 years ago
   - ○ **B.** The distant future
   - ○ **C.** The present
   - ○ **D.** The time of the Revolutionary War

3. **Which of the following best describes the atmosphere at Shortie's Back Room?**
   - ○ **A.** Formal and stiff
   - ○ **B.** Messy and chaotic
   - ○ **C.** Scary and dark
   - ○ **D.** Casual and hip

Billie left the club and went home. She lay on the couch and tried to think. At some point, she fell asleep. She awoke to find Mr. Craven shaking her by the shoulder and scowling, "Wake up!"

Billie shook her head and squinted. "You look different," she told Mr. Craven. Indeed, he looked much more rat-like than before—if that were possible.

"How did you get in here?" she asked.

"Never mind," Mr. Craven said. "Let's go. I've got you a tryout at Ratkins—it's the biggest club in town."

"Ratkins?" Billie asked.

She had never heard of Ratkins before. It was a horrible place. The walls were dingy. The air was hot and smoky. The customers huddled around small dirty tables, hiding their eyes and muttering. They too seemed rat-like and mean. Onstage, a singer crooned out a terrible, off-key song in a hoarse voice. When he finished, the audience jeered and hooted. They threw trash on the stage.

"How awful," Billie said.

"Shut up!" barked Mr. Craven.

Then, a moment later, Billie found herself jerked onto the stage.

"AND NOW, SOMEBODY NEW," the announcer barked. "GIVE A WELCOME TO ANOTHER ROTTEN SINGER!"

"BOO!" cried the audience. "GET RID OF HER!"

"Hey!" Billie said. "That's not fair! I haven't even started yet."

Somebody pushed her. The audience threw things. The band started to play.

"Sing!" shouted the audience members.

Billie looked out at them. There was no

mistaking it now. They weren't just rat-like. They were a bunch of RATS! Filthy, cruel-eyed creatures that sneered and squealed—and spoke.

"Sing!" they demanded. "Sing or get out!"

A bucket of cold soup was dumped over Billie's head. The audience roared with laughter. Billie looked out and saw Mr. Craven. He was laughing harder than anyone!

Billie tried to sing. But now they were hissing and whooping too loud for anyone to hear. Someone threw a rotten tomato at Billie.

"Stop it!" she cried. But now the rats—and they WERE rats—were gathering around. Their eyes were red. Their teeth were yellow.

She got up to run, but suddenly she fell . . . and then the whole world was swirling round and round until . . .

"Billie! Wake up!" a voice said.

"Baxter?" Billie cried. "Am I glad to see you!"

"Billie," he said. "What's wrong? You look like you've seen a ghost."

Billie looked around. There were no jeering rats, no awful music, no foul smoky air. She was no longer in Ratkins. She was back in her own room.

"I—I must have fallen asleep," she said.

"Come on," Baxter said. "We've got to start practicing. For Shortie's Back Room."

As Billie got ready she wondered if it had all been a dream. There, on the table, was Mr. Craven's card: B. CRAVEN, PRESIDENT, RODENT ENTERTAINMENT.

"Where'd you get this?" Baxter asked.

"I found it on the sidewalk," Billie said.

And with that, she tore up the card and threw it in the wastepaper basket. **THE END**

---

4. **What is the setting when Mr. Craven awakens Billie?**
   - ○ **A.** Shortie's Back Room
   - ○ **B.** A club called Ratkins
   - ○ **C.** Billie's hotel room
   - ○ **D.** Billie's house

5. **Where does Mr. Craven take Billie?**
   - ○ **A.** Shortie's Back Room
   - ○ **B.** A club called Ratkins
   - ○ **C.** Billie's hotel room
   - ○ **D.** The offices of Rodent Entertainment

6. **Which of the following best describes Ratkins?**
   - ○ **A.** Hot, dirty, and filled with rude creatures
   - ○ **B.** Hip, modern, and filled with happy people
   - ○ **C.** Large and airy with high ceilings and big windows
   - ○ **D.** Frightening and supernatural

7. **Is Ratkins real?**
   - ○ **A.** Yes
   - ○ **B.** No
   - ○ **C.** It is real only within the context of the story.
   - ○ **D.** It's impossible to tell if it is real or a setting for Billie's dream.

8. **You're the author of *Strangeville: A Guide to the Most Interesting Places*. On a separate sheet of paper, write two entries for the "clubs" chapter—one for Shortie's Back Room and the other for Ratkins. Describe the settings with as much detail as possible.**

Tales From the Telephone: True Horror

An **Author's Purpose** Spooky Story

An **author's purpose** is his or her reason for writing. When you write a shopping list, your purpose is to remind yourself what you need when you're at the store. When you write a ghost story, your purpose is to terrify—and to entertain. Most authors have more than one purpose. What is the author's purpose in this strangely scary telephone tale?

List of Characters

MADGE	**FRANK**
VOICE	**ROBOT**

Welcome to *Tales From the Telephone*, the world's only newsletter featuring actual telephone calls made by real people just like you. Today we focus on Madge Fackley. When Madge placed the call you're about to read, she had just bought a new Potco pot. The handle was loose. To get help, Madge dialed 1-800-POTCO. We present to you a word-for-word transcript of Madge's actual conversation. Here's a warning: This call may terrify you. If you have the guts, listen in.

MADGE: Hello?

VOICE: Welcome to Potco International. Your call is very important to us. For English, press 1. For Spanish, press 2. For dolphin or chimpanzee language, press 3. For gibberish, press 4. To hear somebody mumbling and coughing, press 5.

Madge presses 1.

VOICE: Your call is very important to us. All of our lines are busy at this time. Please wait for the next available representative.

Forty minutes pass.

FRANK: Hello, and welcome to the customer service line for Potco International. This is Frank Zilch. How many I help you?

MADGE: Oh, thank goodness I finally reached somebody!

FRANK: Your call may be monitored for security reasons.

MADGE: Okay. But I just wanted to ask a question.

FRANK: For questions, press 1. For answers, press 2. For questions without answers, press 3. For answers without questions, press 4. For neither questions nor answers, press 5. Or, please stay on the line to hear some elevator music.

Madge presses 1.

VOICE: Thank you for calling the Potco Question Line. Your call is very important. To speak to a representative who knows nothing about your problem, press 1. To speak to a representative who knows nothing about other problems, press 2. To speak to a representative who doesn't even know his or her name, press 3. To speak to a robot, press 4.

Madge presses 4.

VOICE: To speak to a robot who knows nothing about your problem, press 1. To speak to a robot that just repeats the same phrase over and over again, press 2. To be put on hold for another forty minutes, press 3.

Madge presses 1. Forty minutes pass.

ROBOT: Hello, and welcome to the Potco Robot Help Line. Your call is very important. All of our robots are currently on lunch break right now. To leave a message for a robot to call you back as soon as pigs have wings, please press 5 now, or stay on the line for the next available robot . . .

For more telephone terror, look for next week's issue of this newsletter, *Tales From the Telephone*. To subscribe or to share your own telephone travails, call us at 555-FONE. For subscriptions, press 1. To tell your tale, press 2. And remember, at *Tales From the Telephone* your call is always very, very important to us.

THE END

1. **What does the author's main purpose appear to be in this story?**
   ○ **A.** To criticize pot makers
   ○ **B.** To criticize Madge
   ○ **C.** To criticize automated phone systems
   ○ **D.** To criticize the U.S. government

2. **What other purpose does the author have?**
   ○ **A.** To entertain
   ○ **B.** To inform
   ○ **C.** To describe
   ○ **D.** To make an excuse

3. **To communicate purpose, the author uses which literary devices?**
   ○ **A.** Logic and persuasion
   ○ **B.** Humor and irony
   ○ **C.** Rhythm and rhyme
   ○ **D.** Allusion and symbolism

4. **Which outward tone does the author use for the voices that speak to Madge?**
   ○ **A.** A harsh tone
   ○ **B.** A pleasant tone
   ○ **C.** A biting tone
   ○ **D.** A scary tone

5. **What does the author want readers to think the voice really means when it says, "Your call is very important"?**
   ○ **A.** Your call is important.
   ○ **B.** Your call is somewhat important.
   ○ **C.** Your call is not important.
   ○ **D.** Other people's calls are unimportant.

6. **Which of the following is evidence of the author's attitude?**
   ○ **A.** The polite words of the voice
   ○ **B.** The ridiculous choices that the phone voices give Madge
   ○ **C.** The helpfulness of people that Madge gets on the phone
   ○ **D.** The fact that Madge bought a pot

7. **Some of the choices that are given to Madge are dead ends or make no sense. The author is trying to show that callers like Madge often feel**
   ○ **A.** helpless.
   ○ **B.** well taken care of.
   ○ **C.** pleased.
   ○ **D.** frightened.

8. **Imagine that you are Madge. On a separate sheet of paper, write a complaint letter to Potco International describing your experience and asking for service. Use as much humor and irony as you like.**

Problems Facing Young People Today:

An Editorial by Maxwell Bile

A **Fact vs. Opinion** Spooky Story

Facts can be proven true. This is a fact: *The sky is blue.*
Opinions express the way people feel about things.
Here's an opinion: *Ghosts are terrifying.* This odd
newspaper column expresses a weird opinion about
today's youth. And that's a fact—or is it?

Hello, my name is Maxwell Bile and I'm the president of AWFUL (Angry With Foolish Unhealthy Lifestyles)*. I'd like to take a moment to speak about something that is very important to all of us: our children.

Recently, I've noticed some disturbing new trends in our society. Take music, for example. Our young people are being bombarded with nonstop messages about LOVE.

Now don't get me wrong. Love is an important emotion—for puppies, kittens, turtledoves, and other animals. But for people? Give me a break!

These love songs on the radio are poisoning our children, I tell you! But in my opinion they're small potatoes when you compare them with the real culprit in the situation. That's right, I'm talking about Hollywood.

* In fact, Mr. Bile is the only member of the group.

---

1. **Which of these is a fact?**
   - ○ **A.** Maxwell Bile is the president of AWFUL.
   - ○ **B.** Maxwell Bile has some weird ideas.
   - ○ **C.** Maxwell Bile has some great ideas.
   - ○ **D.** Love is for puppies only.

2. **Which of these is an opinion?**
   - ○ **A.** Many young people listen to music.
   - ○ **B.** Love is not an important emotion for people.
   - ○ **C.** Maxwell Bile is the president of AWFUL.
   - ○ **D.** You can hear love songs on the radio.

3. **What in the title of this piece tells you it will probably express an opinion?**
   - ○ **A.** The word *editorial*
   - ○ **B.** The name *Maxwell Bile*
   - ○ **C.** The word *problem*
   - ○ **D.** The words *young people*

4. **Which of these is not an opinion?**
   - ○ **A.** AWFUL is a ridiculous organization.
   - ○ **B.** AWFUL stands for "Angry With Foolish Unhealthy Lifestyles."
   - ○ **C.** AWFUL promotes some wrong-headed ideas.
   - ○ **D.** Maxwell Bile is an excellent writer.

5. **Maxwell Bile is trying to persuade his audience to think a certain way. Which of these opinions matches what Bile is trying to communicate?**
   - ○ **A.** Love songs are poisoning young people.
   - ○ **B.** Love songs are helping children get along in the world.
   - ○ **C.** Love songs are making money for the people who sing them.
   - ○ **D.** Love songs make no sense.

What's wrong with Hollywood? Let me turn the question around: Have you been to a teen movie lately? Some of them make your skin crawl.

Some of them are completely devoid of good taste.

Some of them even make you nauseous!

Unfortunately, for every "good" movie they put out that makes you sick to your stomach, you'll find a half-dozen that do the opposite. They're full of smiling characters, sunny situations, and get this: HAPPY ENDINGS!

Now there are many things that are truly harmful in the world, but none do half the damage of a happy ending. Think of the warped view kids get of the world: Things work out, people can be good and happy, and so on. No screaming. No gore or slime. No dark, dank, and gloomy locales. Nothing sick or twisted. I ask you: Is THIS how we want our kids to grow up?

In conclusion, if you're like me and want to put a stop to all this cheeriness, please contact AWFUL, Angry With Foolish Unhealthy Lifestyles.

Please help.

Not for yourself.

But for the sake of our children.

6. **In Maxwell Bile's opinion, what is wrong with Hollywood?**
   - ○ **A.** It produces movies with bad taste.
   - ○ **B.** It produces movies with happy endings.
   - ○ **C.** It produces movies that are gory and gloomy.
   - ○ **D.** It produces movies that are too long.

7. **In Maxwell Bile's opinion, how do movies warp young people's values?**
   - ○ **A.** By making them think that the world is a cold, cruel place
   - ○ **B.** By making them think that it takes hard work to get ahead in the world
   - ○ **C.** By making them think that problems can be solved in the world
   - ○ **D.** By making them think money is the most important thing

8. **On a separate sheet of paper, write a response to Maxwell Bile's editorial. Make sure your opinion is clear. Be funny or serious.**

The Dirt: A Horror World Gossip Column

by Nintendo Flint

A **Compare and Contrast** Spooky Story

When you **compare and contrast**, you're identifying how things are alike and different. Comparing is showing how two things are alike; contrasting is showing how two things are different. It even applies in the spooky world. To see how, check out this page from an otherworldly celebrity gossip column.

Greetings from "The Dirt," the column that gets you the true dirt on the biggest stars, no matter how deep we need to dig. I'm Nintendo Flint, your loyal lurid reporter.

Now this week's dish.

What's this I hear about Clovina, the Exotic Snake-Woman? Has she dumped the Headless Horseman and gone gaga for the Invisible Man?

The two—Clovina and Invisible—were spotted together at the Mummy's big birthday bash on Friday the 13th. (Or at least *she* was seen; the Invisible Man is a bit hard to spot, if you know what I mean!)

If you ask me, the Headless Horseman was never right for Clovina. I mean, let's face it, she's basically levelheaded, while the Horseman is the type who always seems to lose his head just at the wrong time, if you know what I'm talking about!

This doesn't mean the Invisible Man will be much of an improvement for Clovina. Personally, I don't know what Clo sees in the fellow. For that matter, I don't know what ANYONE sees in him!

And here's a tasty tidbit. Guess what the Incredible Hunk gave the Mummy for a birthday gift? A big hunk of junk! Talk about cheap. The Mum-ster was reported to be furious. "What's with that guy?" he asked. "He's always passing out hunks of things. Why couldn't he just give me a box of chocolate-covered maggots? That's what I wanted."

After the Mummy's party ended, everyone hopped over to the Gloomer Paloomer Theater to see *Greasy Grimy Gopher Guts*, the new movie starring the Spineless Jellyfish and the Brain. If you ask this reporter, the Jellyfish gave a rather weak and spineless performance in the film. The Brain, on the other hand, was magnificent—cool and intelligent. I would almost describe her as "cerebral" if I didn't know better.

---

1. **Compare the Headless Horseman to the Invisible Man. How are the two similar?**
   - ○ **A.** They both ride horses and their faces are well known.
   - ○ **B.** They both like Clovina and their faces are not seen.
   - ○ **C.** They both dislike Clovina and their faces are well known.
   - ○ **D.** They both fought wars.

2. **Contrast Clovina to the Headless Horseman. How are the two different?**
   - ○ **A.** Clovina is levelheaded, while the Horseman is not.
   - ○ **B.** Clovina always loses her head while the Horseman is levelheaded.
   - ○ **C.** Clovina is invisible and the Horseman is visible.
   - ○ **D.** Clovina is visible and the Horseman is invisible.

3. **Contrast the columnist's opinion of the performance given by the Spineless Jellyfish to that of her opinion of the Brain's performance.**
   - ○ **A.** She thought the Brain performed well and the Jellyfish performed poorly.
   - ○ **B.** She thought the Jellyfish performed well and the Brain performed poorly.
   - ○ **C.** She thought they both gave bad performances.
   - ○ **D.** She thought they both gave good performances.

4. **The Hulk gave the Mummy a birthday gift. Contrast the gift the Mummy got with the one he wanted.**
   - ○ **A.** The Mummy got exactly what he wanted.
   - ○ **B.** The Mummy got a hunk of junk but he wanted chocolate-covered maggots.
   - ○ **C.** The Mummy got chocolate-covered maggots but he wanted a hunk of junk.
   - ○ **D.** The Mummy got a hunk of junk but he wanted a puppy.

emember you heard it here first: Wolf Man and the She Wolf are expecting! That's right, a litter is on the way, the stork is at the door, if you know what I mean. Wonder what the little pups are going to look like? Let me guess—kind of hairy with big fangs?

And finally, this just in. There's been a terrible accident—Suzy the Big Purple Dinosaur was run over by a truck driven by the Fly! But never fear—she's only a stuffed animal, for goodness sake. She just lost a little sawdust. NBD! No Big Deal! She's been restuffed! She looks fabulous and she's singing as cheerfully as ever—much to the disappointment of all those people who find her annoying. (Please note: This columnist is not one of those people!)

And speaking of Suzy and the Fly—they've been hanging out quite a bit lately. The accident seems to have brought them together. What a couple! She's a dinosaur, he's an insect! She sings annoying songs, he buzzes annoyingly in people's ears! She's attracted to fancy dinners, while all he wants is to land on your plate! Come to think of it, maybe the two have more in common than you think!

Finally, I'd just like to send out some brief howdy-do's to some of my good pals out there. To the Thing—whatever you are—I love you, man! You're the best. Keep up the good work, whatever it is that you are, and whatever it is that you actually do.

Ditto for the Blob—don't ever change, you big, ugly chunk of formless, featureless protoplasm!

Also, happy anniversary to the Creature from the Black Lagoon. Keep on crawling, partner!

And as for the Boogeyman, the Slimeball, the Wicked Witch of the West, and the Evil Clown—I wish you all well, my friends, in whatever dark corners you lurk.

Until next week, this is Nintendo Flint saying so long and happy haunting, everyone.

---

5. **Compare Suzy the Dinosaur with the Fly. How are the two similar?**
   - **A.** They're both purple.
   - **B.** They both annoy some people.
   - **C.** They're both insects.
   - **D.** They're both stuffed animals.

6. **How does Nintendo's gossip column *compare* with a "typical" gossip column?**
   - **A.** They both report celebrity news.
   - **B.** They both report serious national news.
   - **C.** They are both very serious.
   - **D.** They both report on fictional creatures.

7. **How does Nintendo's gossip column *contrast* with a "typical" gossip column?**
   - **A.** Nintendo's column is accurate; typical columns are inaccurate.
   - **B.** Nintendo's column is well written; typical columns are poorly written.
   - **C.** Nintendo's column is longer than typical columns.
   - **D.** Nintendo's column reports on fictional characters; typical columns report on real celebrities.

8. **Choose two celebrities—one who you like and one who really annoys you. Write a paragraph comparing and contrasting the two celebrities.**

Nasty Little Monster

A **Sequence of Events** Spooky Story

Sequencing is putting events in order. In this tale of a very frightened kid, pay close attention to what happens when—in other words, the sequence of events.

Billy Barrigan was afraid of scary movies. And scary books. Not to mention scary TV shows, scary comics, and scary backs of cereal boxes.

He also was afraid of heights, water, caves, vampires, elevators, dogs, the dark, chicken nuggets, math tests, ponies, lawn mowers, and even birthday cakes!

Come to think of it, there wasn't much that Billy wasn't afraid of.

Except for magic lamps.

"Aha!" Billy said, when he found a magic lamp in an old basement. "Maybe there'll be a genie in here."

Actually, it was more of a jar than a lamp. And when Billy rubbed it, what popped out was more of a ghoul than a genie. It was a Nasty Little Monster.

"*BRA-A-A-H!*" shouted the Nasty Little Monster, in a nasty little voice.

"Yeeks!" cried Billy.

Though the monster was no more than three inches tall, it was still enough to give Billy a big scare. And when the monster scared someone, a strange thing happened. The monster grew!

"*BRA-A-A-A-H!*" shrieked the monster, who had now grown to about six inches.

This six-inch-tall monster was twice as scary as the three-inch-tall monster, so Billy shouted, "Yikes!" this time in a slightly louder voice.

And this louder voice made the Nasty Little Monster grow again. Now he was 12 inches tall—a whole foot!

"Yowks!" cried Billy, a bit more scared than he was before.

Of course, all this did was make the monster grow again. Now he was two feet tall, the size of a medium-sized dog, only he was meaner and nastier than any dog.

"*BRA-A-A-A-A-H-H-HHH!*" shouted the medium-sized monster.

"YOYKS!" wailed Billy, who was getting ever more scared.

This went on for quite some time. The monster grew. And Billy got scared. So the monster grew again. And Billy got even more scared.

It kept on going until the monster was a full 16 feet tall.

"*BRA-A-H-H-H-H!*" shouted the gigantic monster, who was now so big that he would have scared anyone.

"Please," begged Billy. "You're scaring the daylights out of me. Tell me what you want, you Big Ugly Monster."

"What I want is to go back to my lamp," said the Big Ugly Monster. "But now I'm too big to fit in there."

"What will make you smaller?" asked Billy.

"All I can tell you," said the Big Ugly Monster, "is that fear is in your mind. If you control your fear, you can control the size of your monsters."

"Hmm," said Billy.

"Without your fear I am quite small," said the Big Ugly Monster. "Nasty, but small."

"Hmm," Billy said again.

Then it occurred to Billy that the monster was not so scary after all. "You don't scare me," he said.

And with that, the monster started to shrink. From 16 feet tall, he shrank down to eight feet.

"Hey! The monster was right! I really can control my fear," Billy thought.

"*BRA-A-A-H-H-HHH!*" the monster said.

"Big deal!" said Billy.

And the monster shrank down to four feet.

"*BRA-A-A-H-H-HHH!*" said the monster.

"Ha!" said Billy.

They kept on doing this until the Big Ugly Monster was no longer big. In fact, he was exactly three inches tall again, and ready to jump back into his lamp.

"Wait!" cried Billy. "Before you go, I want to thank you."

"What? You want to thank me?" said the Nasty Little Monster. "I'm a nasty little monster. No one has ever thanked me before in my life!"

"But you helped me see that I can control the size of my monsters," said Billy.

"I did?" asked the Nasty Little Monster. Then he thought about it. "Hey, you're right," he said. "Maybe I'm not such a nasty monster after all."

And with that, I'd like to say that the Nasty Little Monster turned into a nice genie and lived in the lamp forevermore, helping people and giving them three wishes.

But that didn't happen.

The monster returned to his lamp, and Billy returned to the real world. Nothing changed, except Billy found that he was no longer afraid of such things as caves and scary movies*.

And did the monster learn anything? Not really. What did you think this was? Some kind of fairy tale?

THE END

* Chicken nuggets, however, are nothing to fool with!

---

1. **After Billy rubs the lamp,**
   - ○ **A.** the monster shrinks.
   - ○ **B.** the monster grows.
   - ○ **C.** he becomes very frightened.
   - ○ **D.** the monster appears.

2. **Billy grows more frightened and then the monster**
   - ○ **A.** gets smaller.
   - ○ **B.** gets bigger.
   - ○ **C.** attacks him.
   - ○ **D.** goes away.

3. **Billy begins to see that fear is something that he can control after the monster**
   - ○ **A.** first scares him.
   - ○ **B.** begins to grow.
   - ○ **C.** begins to shrink.
   - ○ **D.** comes out of the bottle.

4. **Which of these events happens after the monster goes back into the bottle?**
   - ○ **A.** The monster tells Billy that he controls his own fear.
   - ○ **B.** Billy laughs at the monster.
   - ○ **C.** The monster begins to shrink.
   - ○ **D.** Billy finds he is no longer afraid of caves and scary movies.

5. **Imagine that the story is acted out as a play. You see a sixteen-foot monster on stage. What part of the show are you seeing?**
   - ○ **A.** The beginning
   - ○ **B.** The end
   - ○ **C.** The middle
   - ○ **D.** It's impossible to answer with the information given.

6. **Imagine that the story is acted out as a play. You see a one-foot monster on stage. Which detail would help you figure out whether you are seeing the beginning or the end of the story?**
   - ○ **A.** The way Billy responds to the monster's roar
   - ○ **B.** The length of the monster's tail
   - ○ **C.** The loudness of the monster's roar
   - ○ **D.** The brightness of the stage lights

7. **What is the correct sequence of events?**
   1. **The monster tells Billy he can control his own fear.**
   2. **Billy watches in horror as the monster grows larger and larger.**
   3. **The monster comes out of the lamp.**
   4. **The monster shrinks and goes back into the lamp.**

   - ○ **A.** 1, 3, 2, 4
   - ○ **B.** 2, 3, 1, 4
   - ○ **C.** 3, 2, 1, 4
   - ○ **D.** 3, 1, 2, 4

8. **Pick an interesting story from your own life. First, break it down into events. On a separate sheet of paper, make a list of four main events in the story. Make sure they're in chronological (time) order. Then, write a paragraph telling the story. In the story, use some of these words: *first, next, then, before, after, when,* and *finally*.**

The Ghost Who Didn't Believe
A **Cause and Effect** Spooky Story

Forget about ghouls and evil spirits for a moment and think about **cause and effect**. The real world—the one you live in—is a logical place. Things happen for a reason. The reason is the cause. And causes create effects—or results. Now, see how it applies in this unusual ghost story.

There was once a ghost named Wanda who led a happy life. Wanda slept all day. At night, she came out and haunted a creaky old house.

No people ever came to the house, so Wanda had a great time flying around, making spooky noises, and playing with her friends.

After they got done haunting for the evening, Wanda and the others liked to sit in front of the fireplace and tell People Stories. Wanda always had lots of questions about people, because she had never seen one.

"What are people like?" she always asked.

Everyone agreed that people were quite horrible. For one thing, they were solid, not at all like ghosts. For another, they didn't moan and they couldn't fly. Also, you couldn't see through people, they didn't glow, and they preferred day to night, and bright light to darkness.

"How strange," Wanda thought. But the strangest thing of all was that people hated ghosts. When they saw ghosts, people would scream and do all sorts of crazy things to try to destroy them.

"And that means they're scared of us," an older ghost explained to Wanda.

"How awful!" Wanda said. "I don't believe in people."

The others laughed when Wanda said this.

"I don't think people are real," Wanda added. "I've never seen a person. I'll believe in them when I see them."

The others tried to change her mind, but Wanda wouldn't budge. No matter what they said, Wanda still would not believe that people existed.

"People are just a fairy tale," she said. "We ghosts just made them up to scare ourselves on sunny days."

And so it went. After a while, Wanda became known as the Ghost Who Didn't Believe in People.

---

1. **EFFECT: Wanda didn't believe that people were real.**
   CAUSE:
   ○ **A.** Wanda had never seen a person.
   ○ **B.** Wanda read books that said people weren't real.
   ○ **C.** Wanda was afraid of people.
   ○ **D.** Wanda believed in vampires.

2. **CAUSE: The ghosts noticed that people screamed when they saw them.**
   EFFECT:
   ○ **A.** The ghosts thought that people liked them.
   ○ **B.** The ghosts thought that people were afraid of them.
   ○ **C.** The ghosts thought that people were not afraid of them.
   ○ **D.** The ghosts thought humans screamed all the time.

Then one day Wanda woke up a little early and went out into the garden. There, she saw a butterfly flitting by and chased it. The butterfly landed on a flower, and seconds later, a net came down, capturing it. And Wanda was in the net, too. Holding on to the handle of the net was a strange creature.

"Who are you?" asked Wanda, floating easily out of the net. "Are you a ghost?"

The creature laughed. "My name's Jeanette," said the creature. "I'm a girl, and I don't believe in ghosts."

"Well, that's funny, because I'm a ghost myself," Wanda said, "and I don't believe in people!"

The two looked at each other. Both were afraid, but neither was too afraid. Was Jeanette really a person? She did look solid, Wanda thought. She didn't glow and she didn't seem to be able to fly.

"But you can't be a person," Wanda said. "You aren't horrible. And why aren't you screaming? Why aren't you doing crazy things to try to destroy me?"

"Because I like you," Jeanette said. "I'm sorry I netted you! Do you want to be friends?"

"Sure," Wanda said, smiling. Soon Jeanette convinced Wanda that she was a person—a nice one.

From then on, the two met every day at the same time in the garden. They played, sang songs, and had a lot of fun.

"Are you sure you're a person?" Wanda would often ask Jeanette.

"Are you sure you're a ghost?" Jeanette would say.

Then they would both laugh.

This went on. Over time, the Ghost Who Didn't Believe in People began to admit she'd been wrong.

"OK, I'll admit that people do exist," Wanda said to her ghost friends. "But they aren't at all the way we talk about them in our stories."

"Now how would a young ghost like you know that?" the other ghosts would say.

"Oh, I don't know," Wanda said. "It's just a hunch."

THE END

3. **CAUSE: Wanda followed a butterfly.**
   EFFECT:
   - ○ **A.** Wanda got caught in a spiderweb.
   - ○ **B.** Wanda got interested in butterflies.
   - ○ **C.** Wanda got caught in a butterfly net.
   - ○ **D.** Wanda got in trouble.

4. **EFFECT: At first, Wanda couldn't believe Jeanette was a person.**
   CAUSE:
   - ○ **A.** Jeanette seemed horrible.
   - ○ **B.** Jeanette didn't seem horrible.
   - ○ **C.** Jeanette was also afraid of people.
   - ○ **D.** Jeanette was solid.

5. **CAUSE: Jeanette said she wanted to be friends with Wanda.**
   EFFECT:
   - ○ **A.** Wanda screamed.
   - ○ **B.** Jeanette screamed.
   - ○ **C.** Jeanette gave Wanda the butterfly.
   - ○ **D.** Wanda was nice to Jeanette.

6. **CAUSE: Wanda and Jeanette became friends.**
   EFFECT:
   - ○ **A.** They were both ghosts.
   - ○ **B.** They played and sang together.
   - ○ **C.** They were frightened of each other.
   - ○ **D.** Wanda became a person.

7. **EFFECT: Wanda changed her mind about people.**
   CAUSE:
   - ○ **A.** She came to know Jeanette's whole family.
   - ○ **B.** She heard some new stories about people.
   - ○ **C.** She got to know Jeanette.
   - ○ **D.** She saw a convincing movie.

8. **People tell ghost stories, so it stands to reason that ghosts tell people stories! On a separate sheet of paper, write a scary people story that ghosts might tell while sitting around a campfire. In your story, show at least one thing that causes ghosts to get**

Answer Key

Tale No. 1:

The Bijou Ghost (p. 6)

1. C	5. C
2. B	6. B
3. D	7. D
4. C	8. Answers will vary.

Tale No. 2:

Love Potion Commotion (p. 9)

1. A	5. A
2. D	6. B
3. C	7. C
4. C	8. Answers will vary.

Tale No. 3:

The Next Step: Scare Radio (p. 12)

1. C	5. D
2. B	6. A
3. B	7. D
4. A	8. Answers will vary.

Tale No. 4:

The Toothbrush (p. 15)

1. B	5. A
2. B	6. C
3. A	7. B
4. C	8. Answers will vary.

Tale No. 5:

The Ugly Druckling (p. 18)

1. A	5. B
2. A	6. A
3. C	7. C
4. D	8. Answers will vary.

Tale No. 6:

The Horrible Green Creature (p. 21)

1. B	5. C
2. C	6. B
3. B	7. C
4. D	8. Answers will vary.

Tale No. 7:

The House on Plum Street (p. 24)

1. C	5. C
2. A	6. B
3. B	7. D
4. D	8. Answers will vary.

Tale No. 8:

The Hideous Blob's Amazing Comeback (p. 27)

1. B	5. A
2. B	6. B
3. A	7. C
4. D	8. Answers will vary.

Tale No. 9:

The Butcher and His Wife (p. 30)

1. B	5. A
2. A	6. B
3. D	7. A
4. B	8. Answers will vary.

Tale No. 10:

The Three Ghosts of Lucy Bly (p. 33)

1. A	5. A
2. D	6. D
3. B	7. A
4. B	8. Answers will vary.

Tale No. 11:

Ask Aunt Doty: An Advice Column for the Supernaturally Inclined (p. 36)

1. D	5. D
2. A	6. D
3. C	7. D
4. B	8. Answers will vary.

Tale No. 12:

The Choice (p. 39)

1. D	5. A
2. B	6. D
3. C	7. D
4. C	8. Answers will vary.

Tale No. 13:

A Really Bad Hair Day (p. 42)

1. B	5. B
2. C	6. C
3. D	7. D
4. C	8. Answers will vary.

Tale No. 14:

Ratkins! (p. 45)

1. A	5. B
2. C	6. A
3. D	7. B
4. D	8. Answers will vary.

Tale No. 15:

Tales From the Telephone: True Horror (p. 48)

1. C	5. C
2. A	6. B
3. B	7. A
4. B	8. Answers will vary.

Tale No. 16:

Problems Facing Young People Today: An Editorial by Maxwell Bile (p. 51)

1. A	5. A
2. B	6. B
3. A	7. C
4. B	8. Answers will vary.

Tale No. 17:

The Dirt: A Horror World Gossip Column (p. 54)

1. B	5. B
2. A	6. A
3. A	7. D
4. B	8. Answers will vary.

Tale No. 18:

Nasty Little Monster (p. 57)

1. D	5. C
2. B	6. A
3. C	7. C
4. D	8. Answers will vary.

Tale No. 19:

The Ghost Who Didn't Believe (p. 60)

1. A	5. C
2. B	6. B
3. C	7. C
4. B	8. Answers will vary.

Skills Index

READING SKILLS	Page Number	Tale Number
Analyzing Plot	p. 24	Tale No. 7
Author's Purpose	p. 36 p. 48	Tale No. 11 Tale No. 15
Cause and Effect	p. 9 p. 60	Tale No. 2 Tale No. 19
Compare and Contrast	p. 15 p. 54	Tale No. 4 Tale No. 17
Drawing Conclusions	p. 21	Tale No. 6
Fact vs. Opinion	p. 51	Tale No. 16
Main Idea	p. 12	Tale No. 3
Main Idea/ Supporting Details	p. 27	Tale No. 8
Making Inferences	p. 30	Tale No. 9
Making Predictions	p. 39	Tale No. 12
Point of View	p. 18	Tale No. 5
Reading for Details	p. 6 p. 42	Tale No. 1 Tale No. 13
Sequence of Events	p. 57	Tale No. 18
Understanding Character	p. 33	Tale No. 10
Understanding Setting	p. 45	Tale No. 14

WRITING SKILLS	Page Number	Tale Number
Advice Column Letter	p. 36	Tale No. 11
Apology	p. 33	Tale No. 10
Autobiography/ Sequencing	p. 57	Tale No. 18
Compare-Contrast Essay	p. 15 p. 54	Tale No. 4 Tale No. 17
Complaint Letter	p. 48	Tale No. 15
Descriptive Writing	p. 42	Tale No. 13
Descriptive Writing/ Guidebook	p. 6	Tale No. 1
Dialogue Writing	p. 39	Tale No. 12
Job Description	p. 21	Tale No. 6
Magazine Ad	p. 9	Tale No. 2
Main Idea/Outline	p. 12	Tale No. 3
Movie Magazine Article	p. 27	Tale No. 8
Newspaper Article	p. 24	Tale No. 7
Opinion Writing	p. 51	Tale No. 16
Personal Essay/ Point of View	p. 18	Tale No. 5
Reverse Ghost Story	p. 60	Tale No. 19
Setting	p. 45	Tale No. 14
Thank-You Note	p. 30	Tale No. 9